D1002925

Faith
and
Farewell

When Your Parents Approach
Their Final Days

REV. DR. JACK DiMATTEO

WESTBOW
PRESS
A DIVISION OF THOMAS NELSON
& ZONDERVAN

Unless otherwise noted, Scripture quotations are taken from the Life
Application Bible, New International Version, copyright © 1988, 1989,
1990, 1991 jointly by Tyndale H, Publishers, Inc., Wheaton, Illinois, and by
Zondervan Publishing House, Grand Rapids, Michigan. All rights reserved.

Scripture quotations marked "NRSV" are from the Holy Bible, New
Revised Standard Version, copyright © 1990 by Augsburg Fortress
Publishers, Minneapolis, Minnesota. All rights reserved.

WestBow Press books may be ordered through booksellers or by contacting:

WestBow Press
A Division of Thomas Nelson & Zondervan
1663 Liberty Drive
Bloomington, IN 47403
www.westbowpress.com
1 (866) 928-1240

Because of the dynamic nature of the Internet, any web addresses or links contained in
this book may have changed since publication and may no longer be valid. The views
expressed in this work are solely those of the author and do not necessarily reflect the
views of the publisher, and the publisher hereby disclaims any responsibility for them.

Any people depicted in stock imagery provided by Thinkstock are models,
and such images are being used for illustrative purposes only.
Certain stock imagery © Thinkstock.

ISBN: 978-1-4908-6400-6 (sc)
ISBN: 978-1-4908-6401-3 (hc)
ISBN: 978-1-4908-6399-3 (e)

Library of Congress Control Number: 2014922541

Printed in the United States of America.

WestBow Press rev. date: 1/30/2015

To my dear wife, Kathy, who has been my inspiration
and support through the storms of life

Contents

Acknowledgments

This book began to germinate eighteen years ago when I completed my doctoral studies based on the observation of several families engaged in anticipatory grief. As an interfaith hospice chaplain, I interacted with adult children as they prepared spiritually to lose their parents. Included in this book are actual experiences and conversations with patients and families served by

- the Hospice of New Jersey, Bloomfield, New Jersey;
- the Center for Hope Hospice and Palliative Care, Linden, New Jersey (now in Scotch Plains, New Jersey); and
- Compassionate Care Hospice, Parsippany, New Jersey.

Of course, all names mentioned in this book are changed to preserve confidentiality.

During my doctoral project, I was deeply touched by the families who opened their homes and their hearts to me as I helped them sort through the painful process of saying good-bye to parents who were dying. I observed their family dynamics, their coping strategies, their spiritual practices, and their expressions of grief and sadness. The overarching theme for them was helplessness, in spite of all their efforts to halt the disease progression and prolong the lives of their parents. They, and I, gained great respect for the enormity of life—and death—while acknowledging the true value of "surrender" related to the living-dying interval of aging loved ones.

Well into my fifteenth year of helping other adult children cope with impending losses, it was my turn to say farewell to my own aging parents. This farewell spanned over three years, punctuated by the painful experience of making caregiving decisions for my parents who were experiencing greatly diminished physical strength and reduced cognitive faculties. I recall collaborating with my sister Rhonda as we tried to discover the best ways to improve the quality of our parents' lives while coping with our own internal needs to care for those who once cared for us.

Admittedly, I often became "clinical" with my own parents. The clinical veneer was a safe place for me and a refuge from the flood of my own emotions, which vacillated from sadness to anger, frustration, pity, and everywhere in between before arriving at closure and acceptance. For me, the common denominator became helplessness, as I had witnessed in the expressions of so many of the hospice families—then and now. How frustrating it felt not to be able to orchestrate or engineer my parents' final days due to several medical circumstances that were impossible to manage. I tried to attain the spiritual goal of "letting go" while entrusting all circumstances to God's sovereign will. I didn't always succeed in achieving the letting go part, but I prayed for spiritual serenity as each of my parents passed within a nine-month time frame.

I am deeply indebted to a few people who guided me along the clinical road and/or provided the deep emotional/spiritual nurturing needed throughout that journey. Special thanks to Dr. LeRoy Aden, professor emeritus at the Lutheran Theological Seminary at Philadelphia, for his mentoring of my doctoral project years ago. Thanks also to supportive friends like Rev. Charles Ferreri, Rev. Rick Brunzell, and hospice social worker Julie Krupinski, who listened compassionately and gently offered supportive reassurance. I am grateful to my sister Rhonda who really went all out for our parents and then gave two heartfelt and candid eulogies.

Most importantly, I feel deep gratitude and love for my wife, Kathy, who stood by me, frequently offered a shoulder to cry on, and tolerated my expressions of anger and frustration whenever my parents would not cooperate with health-care professionals who tried to improve the quality of their lives. Kathy also patiently offered support throughout the creation of this book and volunteered for a significant portion of copyediting.

Above all, to God be the glory! If it weren't for those times in my Prayer Chair and those quiet early morning Bible studies, I do not know how I could have coped through the process of saying good-bye to two of the most influential people in my life: Mom and Dad. By the grace of God, I made the tiring yet rewarding spiritual journey to help usher my parents from this world to the next.

Likewise, by the grace of God, you will also grow and learn as you spiritually offer your farewells to those who brought you into this world. God be with you!

Rev. Dr. Jack DiMatteo
December 2014

Introduction

Most of us reach a point in our lives when we realize our parents will not live forever. And for most, this revelation occurs sometime in midlife. What about you? Did you wake up the other day and face the startling reality of your parents' mortality? Were you driving down the road, running on a treadmill, or texting a friend when it suddenly occurred to you that someday, and maybe someday soon, your parents will no longer be around and you will be an "adult orphan"?

Assuming your parents did not die when they were young, and assuming that your parents did not die suddenly from unnatural causes, tragedies, or the like, and assuming even further that this book caught your eye for personal reasons, it is probably safe to conclude the following:

- Your parents are aging and are in the twilight of their lives.
- You are either middle aged or rapidly advancing toward that stage in life.
- You are part of a sandwich generation caught between the caregiving responsibilities of your children and your aging parents.
- You are growing increasingly concerned about your parents' overall well-being.
- You are searching for some spiritual meaning at this time in your life.

Then this book is for you!

This book is dedicated to adult children who are witnessing their parents' steady, certain advancement toward death, either through the effects of life-limiting illnesses or the natural aging process.

If you find yourself in this station of life, then no doubt you are trying your best to cope with the approaching death of one or both of your parents. You may be feeling helpless, depressed, overwhelmed, or generally ill equipped to address this delicate time in life while envisioning some form of graceful farewell to the people who have had a tremendous impact on your entire life: your parents!

My Reality

The reality of my parents' mortality hit home for me when my parents became octogenarians. Though my parents were steadily declining physically and cognitively over the years prior to this time, it was as if the mortality switch was instantly flipped to "terminal" once my parents entered the decade of their eighties. Suddenly, as if overnight, there were more doctor appointments, more aches and pains (theirs and mine), more medical procedures, and more contacts from me just to check in to ensure that all was well in their world. There were disagreements between me and my parents regarding how they were to live, where they were to live, with whom they were to live, etc. All the while, I observed each of my parents slipping into a downward spiral from which they would never, ever recover.

My parents' tailspin was indicated by their growing physical weakness, their inability to make simple decisions, their occasional stubbornness, and their propensity to cling to outdated ideologies that were no longer pragmatic or even logical for their stage in life. I discovered my parents waffling between the desires to exert their authority as parents on the one hand and the occasional moments of childlike innocence and dependency on the other hand. They were scared, and I was scared, by a future that promised further deterioration and decline while necessitating critical end-of-life decisions that previously seemed far too distant to even imagine or consider.

During that tumultuous time, I found solace and consolation through prayer, meditation, Scripture readings, exercise, and an occasional good cry. As you will discover from my story, shared in this book, there were days when I seriously wondered how I would approach each new day without falling apart and just giving up. There were frustrating days spent consulting with physicians, planning appropriate care structures, negotiating with insurance companies, conversing with social workers, telephoning agencies, and leaving phone messages for my sister, all the while praying fervently for the spiritual strength to address my parents' personal issues as they declined rapidly over a short period of time.

There were times when caring for my parents became a full-time job, on top of my real full-time job, and in addition to my other full-time job of raising my kids. I will acknowledge now that it was a crazy time in my life as the emotional roller coaster spun out of control on a daily basis. In retrospect, no wonder I felt constantly fatigued and in perpetual need of a vacation!

During the time when my parents demanded more of my attention, I had been serving a ministry as an interfaith hospice chaplain, which meant that I was "clinically" addressing death and dying on a daily basis. By this time, I was in the middle of my second decade of hospice ministry and had loads of clinical training that equipped me to address my own parents' demise. However, when dealing with my own parents, there were several days when I either hid behind the emotion-protecting walls of my clinical acumen or lost rational, objective thought processes altogether while grappling with circumstances regarding end-of-life care that were way beyond my ability to control.

Back then, I discovered that clinical knowledge was a valuable asset in working with my aging parents. Yet when push came to shove (and there were times of shoving), I experienced the push-and-pull, tug-of-war battle between the heart and mind whenever life-changing or life-threatening circumstances demanded prioritizing. My emotions swung faster than a metronome on high speed. My moods changed with the weather, and without the grace of God, I never would have survived.

But I did survive, and now I want to encourage your survival in dealing with the issues you are facing as your parents journey toward the end of their lives. If I could encapsulate my acquired wisdom into one primary piece of advice for you, it would be this: whatever the circumstances you are currently facing, keep telling yourself *if the Lord gets you to it, the Lord will get you through it!*

Your Challenges

There are several spiritual challenges you need to address as your parents age and decline. Your tasks include the following:

- to acknowledge the reality that your parents won't live on this planet forever
- to find closure during the final stretch of your parents' lives
- to say good-bye and to entrust your elderly parents to their eternal destiny
- to *let go* of an intense desire to control every last detail of your parents' final days, months, or years

This book addresses the spiritual dimensions required for addressing these tasks, most notably the task of letting go. It is an essential process for you, a rite of passage, to release yourself from the need to control all circumstances and outcomes, and in doing so, to achieve liberation from the unquenchable desire to orchestrate every last minute of your parents' care. Only in letting go can you fully acknowledge that many circumstances are beyond your control. And relinquishing that control is not the last course of action, but the *primary* strategy. It is a faithful acknowledgment of the Creator's plan, not your own.

The Overall Purpose of This Book

This is not a how-to book but a spiritual guide providing you with suggestions, insights, stories, biblical references, and reflections that will open new opportunities for you to say good-bye to your loved ones with faith in your heart and with the assurance of God's ever-present support in your soul.

Saying farewell to your parents is a spiritual endeavor. In this book, along with my story, I will address the seven spiritual themes that commonly surface during this transitional time:

- authority
- control
- guilt
- loss
- isolation
- anger
- grace

When you open yourself up to explore these themes, you will grow spiritually as you gently usher your parents toward their earthly finish line. I am not suggesting that the process will be carefree and effortless—quite the contrary! I am suggesting, however, that with an open heart and a willingness to allow God's grace to flow through you, the entire journey will become much more meaningful for you and for your aging parents.

This book is written from a Christian perspective and contains several references to the Judeo-Christian Bible. Unless otherwise noted, all Scripture translations are taken from the New International Version of the Bible (NIV).

Consider this book my invitation for you to begin a spiritual journey unlike any other.

Part 1 of this volume outlines the overall spiritual dimensions of saying farewell to your parents. Part 2 offers tips for your spiritual survival during these changing times, with biblical insights to strengthen you in God's Word.

In the pages that follow, you will discover

- **my story**, with the hope that you can make your own personal connections to my experience and discover what it is like for you to say good-bye to an elderly parent;
- **your story**, as you understand your own anticipatory grief and the multitude of emotions that will inevitably influence the manner in which you say good-bye and find closure;
- **our story**, as we discover the spirituality of letting go and learn about the experiences of others who have faithfully, and oftentimes painfully, reached the finish line with their parents; and
- **God's story**, as we reflect on the biblical and theological themes of mortality and death.

I strongly encourage you to embrace the suggested Bible readings to assist your growth in God's Word. Practice these exercises, and read the biblical passages in a concentrated effort to strengthen your daily spiritual walk with God.

By all means, pray before you read each section of this book, pray during your reading, and pray after each reading as you invite the Lord to assist you toward further spiritual enlightenment.

Take Hold of Faith

During this season in life, it is essential that you take hold of faith. It is a time to prepare to say good-bye and a time to embrace the eternal destiny that beckons each of God's children (including your parents) to their heavenly destination.

My personal signature verse that I now invite you to adopt is below.

> Trust in the Lord with all your heart,
> And lean not on your own understanding.
> In all your ways acknowledge him,
> And he will make your paths straight.
>
> Do not be wise in your own eyes;
> Trust the Lord and shun evil.
> This will bring health to your body
> And nourishment to your bones.
>
> —Proverbs 3:5–8

Almost two thousand years ago, St. Paul wrote, "I pray that the eyes of your heart may be enlightened in order that you may know the hope to which he has called you" (Ephesians 1:18). I echo this fervent prayer, that my words coupled with God's grace will help you to open the "eyes" of your heart—to discover the hope that your parents' final days can be lived with dignity and peace while you find spiritual comfort in the journey.

It is time to open this book and start your journey … with your eyes and your soul wide open.

Part 1

Preparing for a Spiritual Farewell

Chapter 1

Is It Time to Let Go?

A woman was climbing the side of a mountain. She was alone, contrary to the advice of anyone even remotely familiar with the art of scaling mountains. As she ascended, she suddenly lost her footing and began tumbling, out of control, down the steep slope. Tumbling faster and faster, she could do nothing to prevent the inevitable ... the out-of-control helpless plunge over the side of a cliff. While she was free falling, she noticed a branch jutting out from an overhang. In one last gasp to save her life, she reached out and successfully grasped hold of that solitary branch. Holding on for dear life, there she was, swinging in midair with nothing above her, and beneath her only an enormous airy cavern beckoning her destruction. "Lord, save me!" she pled with anxious desperation. Immediately, to her surprise and amazement, a heavenly voice came from somewhere "up there." The voice boomed, "Let ... go ... of ... the ... branch." To which the desperate climber replied, "Can I speak to somebody else up there?"

—Author unknown

"Let go ... and let God!" We have all heard that expression. Why then is it so unnatural and uncomfortable for most of us to follow this sound advice when tumbling out of control or when dangling from that last branch of security? Perhaps, we don't heed this advice because it is so counterintuitive to let go, to throw caution to the wind, and to trust completely in the providence of God.

For most of us, there seems to be a built-in, natural resistance to letting go. After all, it is too scary to let go. In fact, it is terrifying, and therein lies the irony, since most of us were instructed from the early days of our childhood to honor the Lord's omnipotence and trust him with every fiber of our being. We were advised to trust unconditionally in the providence of God and not to rely on our own strength or ingenuity during times of despair.

During the early days of toddlerhood, when we first sang "Jesus Loves Me," we discovered the primary task of all Christians: to embrace God's unlimited assurances, to fall into the arms of the Shepherd when times got rough, and to completely trust in the Lord for our saving grace. We heard our pastors encouraging us to turn to Jesus, while the children's sermon addressed squirming, fidgeting, youngsters concerning the truth of God's message "My grace is sufficient for you" (2 Corinthians 12:9). Yes, we were instructed, over and over again, to trust in God with heart, soul, and mind. As the years progressed, we sang fervently and passionately the lyrics of "Leaning on the Everlasting Arms" while the choir chimed in with four-part harmony. The message was clear each Sunday: trust in God. Period!

Yet despite all those years of exposure to grace-filled sermons and hymns beckoning us to trust the Almighty, most of us eventually grew up to possess an extreme aversion toward relinquishing control to anyone or anything. To this day, we often maintain those clenched fists of ours and do not even think of gracefully falling into the protective embrace of God.

Are *You* Able to Let Go? Can *You* Trust God?

So much for the pluralistic Christian recollections. Now, let's get personal: how do *you* feel about all the letting go theology? You know in your heart of hearts that God won't let you down. Chances are you've read the biblical accounts of times when the Lord faithfully answered the prayers of dedicated servants who looked heavenward, pleading for grace and mercy. The Lord sustained them. Are you prepared to be next in line when God showers sustaining blessings your way? Are you prepared to be caught by your loving God when you free-fall from desperate circumstances?

No doubt, you have heard sermons about trust and about faith under fire. Chances are you can recall experiences in your own life when God came to the rescue at just the right moment— when you were at wit's end, in the eleventh hour, with your back against the wall—and then God's grace came flooding in to change circumstances and events for your survival.

Just think back upon your personal history at a time when you thought that life was just too unbearable and you were convinced that there was no logical way to survive the next personal disaster. Wasn't it just then when God spoke to you through an encouraging thought, a prayer-whisper, or the actions of a loving friend, all resulting in an uncanny twist of fate absolutely beyond logical expectation, which landed you back on your feet again? Faith tells you that those saving reversals in your life were those precise times when God's grace mobilized for you. And you learned that there is no such reality as a "coincidence," only a "God incident."

Is It Too Scary to Let Go?

So why then do you find it so unreasonable to let go of some earthly branch of security in favor of God's rescuing hand? Why is it seemingly impossible to loosen the death grip, to let go, and to land safely on the side of faith prepared by the grace of the God who loves you more than you can imagine? Why is it so unnatural to pray "thy will be done" and not "my will be done"?

Let's face up to the reality. Letting go can be the most frightening thing you'll ever experience. I recall a popular youth group exercise in which a volunteer is told to stand upright, with arms at one's side. Then, while maintaining a rigid, upright posture, the volunteer is instructed to fall backward into the arms of two or three "catchers." I've tried this. It is really scary to fall back, without any guarantee of support, while thinking that you are going to crack the back of your head on the floor. But just then, as you are about to hit the floor and your stomach rises into your throat, the catchers do their job and prevent you from winding up in the nearest emergency room. It's a rush of fear and faith, coursing through your entire body. That's precisely what it feels like to let go of all visible support. Fear becomes entangled with faith, and you don't know where one ends and the other begins. What you do discover, however, is the faith-filled relief of being "caught" in your time of helplessness. God is willing to catch you in your moment of terror. Can you let go of earthly supports and trust in that reality?

Is Letting Go an Indication of Failure?

There's another way to explain an aversion toward letting go. Not only is letting go a "trust" thing, but letting go can be perceived as a "loser" thing. Perhaps the thought of surrendering to anything or any being feels kind of wimpy. It may appear to be a defeatist philosophy, this surrendering, as opposed to fighting the good fight. The age-old slogan is "If at first you don't succeed, try, try again." You never hear "If at first you don't succeed, raise the white flag, surrender, fall backward, and hope somebody can catch you!" Let's face it: persistence is encouraged in our society—not resignation.

No doubt, you have admired heroes throughout history who consistently and persistently followed their dreams and did not back down at the first signs of adversity or failure. These heroes continued to press on and are now lauded for their indefatigable spirits. One of my personal heroes is Thomas Edison, who "failed" thousands of times before eventually perfecting the light bulb. Imagine if he just resigned and walked away after the first hundred or so "failures"? Legend has it that later, when asked about why he did not get frustrated after several attempts and "failures," Edison was heard to reply, "If I find ten thousand ways something won't work, I haven't failed. I am not discouraged, because every wrong attempt discarded is just one more step forward."[1] How's that for a positive spin on repeated disappointment?

Now back to you. During adverse circumstances, do you feel that surrendering is wimpy or a form of failure? Do you feel that surrendering is a resignation? Do you feel that surrendering is a premature cop-out on the "If at first you don't succeed" mantra?

From a spiritual perspective, I am not suggesting that surrender represents failure. Quite the contrary. True *spiritual* surrender involves seeking God's wisdom, respecting God's authority, trusting in God's providence, and doing your very best while acknowledging the Lordship of the Omnipotent One who can change any situation in accord with divine will. When facing life's frightening and daunting challenges, it is best to faithfully yield to the One whose wisdom and mercy extend far beyond your intellectual capacity.

Today, you can decide to walk with God every step along the way, not just occasionally or when all other options are exhausted. The psalmist faithfully proclaims, "Cast your cares on the Lord and the Lord will sustain you. God will never let the righteous fall" (Psalm 55:22). If you truly incorporate that statement into a life of faith, then soon you will learn that "letting go of the branch" means intentionally surrendering in faith to the One who will guide you and comfort you, through even the toughest of times. You will get through it, when the Lord leads you to it!

Letting Go in Faith When Your Parents Approach Death

One of the most difficult of all seasons of life involves the process of losing that lifelong parent/child bond. When parents approach death, the adult children face the spiritual reality that a special lifelong bond is about to be severed—forever. There is a conscious awareness that letting go may involve helplessly witnessing those last granules of sand trickle down in the hourglass of time.

Cognitively, everyone knows that all efforts to prevent death or eliminate death are futile. You know that your parents won't live forever. Nonetheless, you may try diligently to manipulate the environment, to alter medications, to change medical care plans, and to seek out every available restorative option in an attempt to buy more time. All this may even affect the way you pray. You might begin telling God what to do rather than trusting in the natural timetable that God has prepared for your aging parents.

Referencing the opening illustration of this chapter, nobody really *wants* to be out of control at a time like this. And neither do you. Especially when cherished parents are declining physically and cognitively. You may sincerely desire to take an active role in managing end-of-life care decisions, and you do not want to feel as if you are tumbling helplessly down the side of the mountain. You do not want to lose the grip on that last branch of support, because after all, there *should* be a more systematic, if not a more directive, way to resolve those final details. You do not want your parents to catapult right through the valley of the shadow of death with the accompanying feeling that there's nothing left to do or that there are no other viable options to sustain life.

So ... What Now?

Let's acknowledge the reality: sometimes, it is excruciatingly painful to witness your parents slowly advancing to the finish line of their earthly lives. You don't know how much time you'll have with them before they die. You don't know what their quality of life will be in those final chapters of their earthly existence. You don't know if they will become senile or demented to the point where they will no longer be able to identify you or to converse with you. You don't know how actively they will participate in their end-of-life decision making or whether they will be so cognitively diminished that you will end up making all the critical end-stage choices for them.

At a time like this, you may not be aware of helpful resources, medical options, or any other ways you can assist your parents in making that hoped-for smooth transition from this world to the next.

Chances are you do not relish feeling powerless or dominated by the irrepressible forces of mortality advancing closer to your parents. You do not want to feel defeated by circumstances—be they medical, physical, financial, spiritual, or otherwise—that will ultimately accelerate a decline resulting in the loss of your parents whom you probably value more than any others in your world.

When Fighting Does Not Prove Beneficial

I have been an interfaith hospice chaplain for the better part of eighteen years. I have personally observed thousands of adult children in their attempts to grapple with the enormity of the impending loss of their parents. In fact, I conducted an entire doctoral project that studied common behavior patterns of adult children when they learned their parents were terminally ill. These adult children were experiencing "anticipatory grief," a clinical term that encapsulates the myriad of emotions commonly experienced in preparation for a loved one's death.

During these times of anticipatory grief, the adult children I observed began to feel the relationship with their parents steadily slipping away. It was precisely during these times of growing despair that most of the adult children fought as hard as they could to preserve the status quo. At times, heroic efforts were expended to stop disease progression and the advancing physical demise of their aging parents. All-out efforts were made to prolong life. For these adult children, the mere thought of letting go and saying good-bye to Mom or Dad seemed far beyond the horizon of reasonable choices.

Not long ago, I witnessed a situation in which a hospice patient was ninety-seven years old, extremely debilitated physically and mentally, weighing about ninety pounds, and unable to move without assistance. This woman's adult child opted for all life-sustaining measures. As power of attorney and health-care proxy, the daughter refused to sign a DNR order (do not resuscitate) even though her mother was receiving hospice care, had a bad heart, and had a medical prognosis of less than six months to live. One day, as predicted, the mother, who was receiving hospice care in a nursing facility, went into cardiac arrest. EMT personnel were called immediately, and the rescue workers began frantically pounding on this women's sternum, breaking several ribs while causing severe trauma for this patient who was slipping away toward death. They intubated her, set up an intravenous line, and whisked her off to the nearest hospital. The ninety-seven-year-old woman died shortly after arriving at the medical center.

One can only imagine the sheer terror and trauma this woman experienced in the final minutes of her life in that ambulance. But it did not have to be that way. There was an alternative option, a choice to allow the woman to drift peacefully away, to entrust this frail soul to her eternal Creator, and to eliminate all trauma and terror in those final moments. But that's not what her daughter wanted. Her daughter wanted all invasive efforts to prolong the life of her fragile, terminally ill, ninety-seven-year-old mother.

Later, when asked why she opted for "heroic measures" as opposed to allowing death to run its natural course, the daughter responded, "Years from now, I don't want to look back on this moment knowing I could have done more yet did nothing."

Can you feel empathy for the daughter? Or do you criticize her actions? Can you imagine the pain that daughter must have felt when contemplating the loss of her dear mother? Can you appreciate the daughter's terror at the mere *thought* of letting go?

I must admit I disagree with the daughter's decisions regarding her mother's end-of-life care. However, I can understand the deep love this daughter had for her dying mother; and I can imagine the overwhelming anticipatory grief this daughter may have felt whenever confronted with the reality of her mother's impending death. Perhaps the anticipatory grief itself clouded logical decision making, resulting in those inappropriate, final emergency choices. In a very real sense, the daughter's choices may have been motivated by an intense fear, the terror of losing her mother forever.

This story illustrates my earlier claim. When confronted with the advancing death of a parent, most adult children opt for a multitude of medical strategies, with the last resort involving letting go or surrendering to God's will.

Going Out with Guns Blazing

In the movie *The Bucket List*, the lead character, Edward Cole (played by actor Jack Nicholson), learns that he has a terminal illness (or "life limiting," as we say in the hospice world). While coming to grips with his unavoidable demise, Edward makes a decision: he's not going to roll over and play dead. He's not going to find a convenient corner of the room, curl up, and resign his fate to the forces of the universe. He's not going to raise the white flag. He's not going to sit around looking at the four walls feeling sorry for himself until death comes knocking.

No! Oh no!

Edward's decided strategy is expressed in a poignant question posed to his newly found friend and hospital roommate. "Don't you want to go out with guns blazing?"[2]

Although this is a relevant illustration from the perspective of the one who is terminally ill, the surrounding family members may also, at one time or another, choose from a panoply of options in favor of "going out with guns blazing." Yet at some point along the journey, there comes the realization that the best and most appropriate strategy is not to fire the guns at will but to trust in God to navigate the journey to the earthly finish line. To borrow a phrase from a once popular country song, it may be time to take a place in the unfamiliar passenger seat, not the driver's seat, and let "Jesus, take the wheel!"

If you are in a relationship with a beloved parent who is terminally ill and/or rapidly aging, it may be time to reflect upon your own version of "going out with guns blazing." What does it mean for you? A fight to the finish? A struggle to the bitter end? Is this what your parents *really* want, or is it more about what you want?

Perhaps you're already in an all-out war with the forces of aging and decay vis-a-vis your parents' steady medical decline. Are the guns still blazing? If so, has that philosophy been rewarding for you? Satisfying? Challenging? Frustrating? Exhilarating? Exhausting? What has been your strategy for "fighting this thing" to the bitter end? What has been your game plan to maintain control, dominance, endurance, and individual fortitude in the face of daunting powers that are indomitably poised to take your loved one away from this world?

Maybe your choice has been to fight even harder. After all, the colossal cancer must be battled head-on with the tenacity of a prizefighter in the midst of a fifteen-round battle, and that harrowing heart disease must be pushed aside with brute force involving the newest medications, state-of-the-art pacemakers, defibrillators, beta-blockers, and the works!

Control, restore, renew!

Later in this book, I will share from personal experience on this issue. I will tell the tale of my own aging parents and my reactions to their demise. There were times when I stumbled and fell. There were times when I did not see the forest for the trees and became ungrounded from previous theologies I thought were firmly moored. There were times I wanted to start the guns a-blazing! In short, there were times when I became emotionally unglued at the prospect of saying that final good-bye. I almost opted for heroic measures, which in retrospect would have been extremely inappropriate and torturously painful for my aging parents.

Observing parents who are inching closer to death is a very draining task. As stated earlier, the temptation is to do everything under the sun to prevent further deterioration and decline. All these actions and strategies are performed genuinely in the name of love— even if they are actions that are later perceived retrospectively to have been unnecessary and/or painful for all parties involved in the drama.

A Dumpty Saga

I invite you to recall the popular nursery rhyme "Humpty Dumpty." You will recall that Humpty had a great fall, and all the king's horses and all the king's men (and women) tried to put Mr. Dumpty back together again. And why not? They loved Mr. Dumpty, didn't they? God forbid if Mr. Dumpty would ever fall apart without the valiant efforts of the king's dedicated staff to prevent the total breakdown and collapse of Humpty's delicate frame.

However, in the aftermath of the Dumpty tragedy, the only thing we can now conclude with any certainty is that, despite the efforts of all the king's horses and all the king's men (and women), Mr. Dumpty was not able to be restored to his old self again. We are to assume that, unlike others in his fairy-tale village, Humpty did not *live happily ever after*. Someday, at some defining moment, the reality of Humpty's mortality became evident to all. Those closest to Humpty had to face the undeniable reality of Humpty's impending death.

Your Predicament

Now, let's return to you. Are you an elderly parent's adult child who has summoned all the king's men (and women) and all the credentialed medical personnel in a desperate effort to put *your* loved one back together again? And in the midst of these heroic efforts, are you still frustrated because all those strategies have done little to stave off further decline and deterioration? Do you resolve to fight even harder for your loved one? Do you clench your fist, grit your teeth, dig in the dirt, scream heavenward, and grind forward, because, after all, "if at first you don't succeed ..."?

Do you bargain with God for bonus time? Do you wait for newer and newer therapies while facing the growing realization that you are becoming exhausted and burned out, if not cynical about the whole meaning of life? Do you curse mortality itself? Do you slip into an existential funk or feel cheated that time has robbed you of remaining experiences you could have enjoyed, or should have enjoyed, with your ailing parents? Do you lose sleep at night while lying in bed, staring at the ceiling and wondering what other options are at your disposal to save the day?

How do you cope with it all while maintaining some semblance of sanity in the process? And where does faith fit in? Is there any room left for hope?

A New Strategy

I'd like to propose a new strategy that involves letting go of the branch to see what God can do. It is a strategy that involves an increasing awareness and respect for the finitude of each human lifespan; a strategy that acknowledges human mortality while affirming the omnipotence of God; a strategy that opens the door for God's will rather than incessantly relying on an egocentric stubbornness that screams, "My way or the highway."

This new strategy is attentive to the voice of the Almighty advising you to "be still, and know that I am God [and you are not God]" (Psalm 46:10).

At this point, a word of clarity is in order. I am not suggesting that children of elderly parents do *nothing* in the wake of natural aging and/or life-limiting circumstances, and by no means am I instructing any reader toward complete resignation without availing oneself of the latest technology that offers greater relief and comfort to an aging parent. However, I am encouraging adult caregivers and care managers to examine the fine lines that separate appropriate, reactive strategies from inappropriate, potentially harmful actions. Micro-managing all caregiving details may produce a result that is burdensome and painful for the aging parents.

For all adult children of the elderly, there needs to be a sober moment of awareness that interrupts the obsessive-compulsive desire to "play God." This precise sober moment involves yielding to the Author of all grace, peace, life, and death.

Toward a Greater Acceptance

Most likely, you are familiar with the landmark studies of the late Elisabeth Kubler-Ross, who examined the psychodynamic reactions of patients who had received terminal diagnoses and who were grappling with the myriad of coping strategies for emotional and spiritual survival.[3] It was Kubler-Ross who clearly identified and articulated the ultimate need for resolution or "acceptance" of circumstances with the final goal of gaining closure, peace, and spiritual finality.

Though the initial studies of Kubler-Ross focused on the reactions/coping strategies of the patients, other peripheral observers, such as adult children, discovered that similar processes were happening with them as well. Caregivers and loved ones learned to cycle through the stages of denial, anger, bargaining, depression, and acceptance too. (And keep in mind that the observing clinicians were the first to indicate that these coping cycles rarely followed a predictable linear progression but vacillated back and forth—along with the ebbs and flows of reactive cognition.)[4]

The challenge for you and all other adult children of aging parents rests with ultimately discovering that Kubler-Ross "acceptance" along with the adoption of a peaceful balance between doing and being. This all leads toward a comfortable resolution that concludes *I've done all that I can do, within reasonable and practical limits.* The challenge beckons a healthy awareness of your behaviors that fall somewhere in the middle of a delineated continuum involving micromanagement on one side of the spectrum and apathy/withdrawal on its opposite side. In other words, the spiritual challenge for end-of-life decision makers is to settle upon a middle ground somewhere between the extreme polarities of authoritarianism and neglect.

Grace … Not Pain

Saying good-bye to your parents does not have to be a gut-wrenching, painful experience. You don't have to struggle to find new medical interventions. You don't have to order heroic measures. Remember, you don't have to resist God's loving call when your parents are invited to enter the heavenly kingdom. In fact, your parents may be more receptive than you when it comes to answering God's invitation to enter their eternal home!

As a hospice chaplain and ordained pastor for several years, I have been at the bedsides of many who were dying. And I have had several experiences in comforting family members who endured the seemingly endless predeath vigils while feeling helplessly and emotionally out of control. Their good-byes were often pain-filled, not faith-filled, in spite of my efforts to introduce prayer and solemnity to the atmosphere. *Your* good-bye does not have to be a spiritually painful rite of passage.

I was present at my own mother's bedside when she crossed over the threshold from this world to the next, and I recall, in those final hours, encouraging my mother to embrace the sleep of death. My words were something like "Mom, you will soon fall asleep, but then you will find yourself awake in God's kingdom. Do not be afraid. The Lord will be with you always."

It took a lot of spiritual strength for me to let go of my mother and entrust her to the angels. But I knew that, for my mother, heavenly paradise was just one breath away—an exhale toward peace for all of eternity.

Although I came to accept and embrace the spiritual awareness of my mother's mortality, it was, nevertheless, emotionally excruciating to say good-bye. That story is told more fully in chapter 4.

My farewell story actually begins, however, with the painful and draining experience of losing my father, who departed from this world just nine months prior to my mother's passing. His story is shared in the following chapter.

Chapter 2

Dad: "My Way Mickey"

Be kind to your kids …
someday they will select your nursing home.
—Author unknown

"Parents are tough to raise these days!" I recall proclaiming to my friend Chuck in a phone conversation years ago. I could envision him smiling in response to my words. If anybody understood that statement, Chuck certainly did. He had the unenviable task of trying to "raise" his mother, who was now exhibiting signs of dementia. According to Chuck, his mother could not remember where she put things, with whom she had spoken the day before, or which medications she did or did not take recently. And all the while, Chuck's mother demanded her independence and insisted on living alone in a nearby senior-living complex. "Yeah, parents are tough to raise; they never seem to cooperate," Chuck retorted.

Through the years, Chuck and I have had supportive phone conversations on a fairly regular basis. Topics have ranged from upcoming sermon ideas (he's a pastor too) to the New York Yankees (our beloved team that has recently failed miserably at situational hitting) to dysfunctional parishioners (there are none of those, are there?). However, back then, our lengthy conversations consistently gravitated back to raising parents, which, for each of us, developed into a never-ending endeavor involving creative care planning and the occasional use of reverse psychology—all in an effort to get passive-aggressive parents to make healthier life choices. The fun never ended.

Whenever I spoke with Chuck, I came to the realization that I was caught in the middle, somewhere between two budding, sometimes rebellious adolescent sons who lived with me and two divorced, recalcitrant parents who each resided an hour's drive away from me. (My parents were divorced from each other for the better part of over twenty years.) I joined millions of other fiftysomethings commonly known as the sandwich generation—sandwiched between raising kids *and* parents.

Dad

My father, Mickey, was in his early eighties when the downward spiral began.

Mickey was a blue-collar US Navy veteran retiree who lived alone for twenty-five years after my mom divorced him. Upon retirement from serving as an inventory clerk at a paper factory, he served as a security guard at the front desk of an office building owned and operated by Larry Holmes, former WBC heavyweight boxing champion. Mickey had an important job and served a critical role in Larry Holmes Enterprises. For years, his primary responsibility consisted of planting himself at the front desk in the lobby and occasionally running out into the parking lot to accost a motorist with "You can't park there! It's reserved!"

Mickey was blessed by the companionship, conversation, and conviviality of attractive female bank tellers who traversed back and forth through the lobby during business hours. The Holmes building housed a bank branch on the first floor. Mickey quickly earned the reputation of the "dirty old man." (Not dirty in the sense of personal hygiene, but dirty from a pornographic mind-set.) He'd flirt with women thirty to forty years his younger. Nobody accused him of sexual harassment because nobody took him seriously—and besides, they all thought he was loveable and cute.

Oh, the cute part? He was kind of charming. He was of Sicilian descent and the spitting image of Yogi Berra, complete with bulbous nose and slightly dropping ears. When he smiled, his eyes would twinkle and his huge grin would reveal a Vince Lombardi–like space between his two front teeth.

Everybody loved Mickey, even the federal judge who occupied one of the office suites upstairs. One time the judge was conversing with Mickey in the lobby and the judge passed gas. Without hesitation, Mickey responded, "Your tone and pitch were superb." To which the judge quickly retorted, "Thank you. I've been taking lessons! How nice of you to appreciate my musical ability!"

Mickey was the straight guy with the judge's humor, but he was best known for his own comedic talent, and could he deliver a joke! Even if the joke originated a hundred years ago and everybody already knew the punch line, Mickey could leave his listeners in stitches. "It was all in the delivery," he boasted.

At Home

The kinda cute, kinda charming Mickey was kinda different and kinda intense in the private confines of his home when nobody was watching. (More will be shared on that subject later in these pages.) He lived in a two-story "apartment" behind a tailor shop. The apartment felt more like a house than an apartment because of the spacious rooms, nine-foot ceilings, wooden columns demarcating the passage between the dining room and living room, four bedrooms, and all. It bears noting that, during the last twenty years of his life at "three fifty-four" (our nickname for the house/apartment corresponding to the address), the refrigerator was brown, the curtains were brown, the kitchen cabinets were brown, the walls were brown, the china was brown, and the microwave was brown. Not by choice. All these things were, at one time, white or beige. They gradually transformed into brown entities due to their incessant exposure to cigarette smoke. The smoke emanated continuously from unfiltered cigarettes, and did that smoke stink!

Mickey was a chain smoker of the old-time variety. Two packs a day. Maybe three. At any given moment, one could walk into three fifty-four and be treated to a real smokehouse environment. I used to joke with a combination of amusement and disgust that all my dad ever consumed was smoked foods: smoked sandwiches, smoked desserts, and smoked candy, all washed down with gallons of smoked coffee.

I hated all the smoke. Mickey smoked at all times and in all places, even when sitting on the john or when shaving. (I know, probably too much information there. But it was actually comical to watch the guy prepare to shave with a face lathered heavily in shaving cream—while a cigarette protruded from his mouth. From the side, it looked like a snowman with a nicotine habit.)

Ironically, it wasn't the smoke or the smoking that eventually killed him. No! Occasional chest X-rays would reveal that he had the lungs of a power swimmer. No kidding! That's freaky, but true. It was all the other stuff that killed him.

Mickey was the poster child for self-neglect. He never, ever exercised or even strolled around the block. For years, he simply stopped scheduling doctor visits, dental visits, and other self-maintenance field trips. My sister Rhonda and I pleaded with him constantly to address his medical issues.

"Dad, we'll drive you to the doctor for a checkup."

"No!"

"We'll take you to the dentist."

"No!"

"How about the eye doctor?"

"No! No! No!"

It got so bad we would offer incentives similar to those one might offer to a little child: a special meal in return for a trip to the optometrist, etc. But his noncompliance was consistent and predictable.

Actually, Mickey had a good excuse for wanting to remain at home: irritable bowel syndrome. That nasty condition could flare up at any time and at any place, without prior warning. Mickey had his share of accidents in which his bowels exploded in the car or when racing up the stairs to the bathroom in response to one of those terrible pre–bowel movement labor pains. Irritable bowel syndrome, combined with intense anxiety about everything, combined for a repetitive cocktail of discomfort and misery.

It was no surprise to anyone that these two conditions—irritable bowel syndrome and chronic anxiety—were inseparable. And in all fairness, Mickey's apparent medical self-neglect was largely blamed on these coexisting realities. He canceled dental appointments and doctor appointments and eventually most social appointments due to the fear of a potential bowel disaster that could flare up while in the dental chair, at the movies, or wherever. In fact, just the anxiety of anticipating an upcoming medical appointment would trigger chronic diarrhea several days in advance of the scheduled date.

After a while, Mickey was terrified of scheduling any appearance outside of his home. What if he embarrassed himself by soiling his pants ... in public?

When most accidents occurred, it wasn't simply a soiling experience; it was an avalanche of watery fecal excrement running down his legs and on to the floor, drenching through the underwear and pants and stinking to high heaven. He was too proud to wear diapers or pull-ups. It was easier to stay home, worry more, and wait for the next intestinal flood gate to burst.

Several decades earlier, Mickey had hemorrhoidal surgery while a sailor during WWII. Numerous proctologists years later would concur that the navy's hemorrhoidal surgery was tantamount to authorized medical butchering. Things got so bad that Mickey could hardly control the anal sphincter muscles at all, accounting for the accidents. Normally, one is able to hold back a strong defecation urge until finding a nearby toilet facility. Not Mickey. His sphincter muscles were so weak he simply could not hold back when the violent urges came upon him like tidal waves. One minute, he would be fine. The next minute, anybody standing nearby could hear a rumbling sound articulating from somewhere deep in Mickey's lower intestine. And then, in the blink of an eye, after the rumbling, the avalanche. How sad. How torturous.

So for years, Mickey lived a semireclusive life, afraid to leave home, afraid to wander too far from a nearby toilet. He only left the house for brief intervals. Then, whenever he did leave the house, the phobia of having an embarrassing bowel accident actually triggered the intestinal irritation. It was a vicious cycle. "There's no cure for this!" Mickey often exclaimed along with his litany of other complaints regarding aches, pains, and various inconveniences.

My Way or the Highway

Now, the stubborn, recalcitrant part. Mickey was told by countless health-care professionals to modify his diet to avoid loose stools and gastrointestinal distress. Each time, Mickey disregarded medical advice in favor of short-term pleasure.

"Forget medical advice. I'm going to have that (greasy) cheese steak ... I like coated fried chicken and that's that ... Who's going to stop *me* from having roast beef sandwiches (dripping with grease)? I don't care if I drop dead. I'm not going to eat crackers the rest of my life."

At the core of the issue was that Mickey had always had a defiance of authority figures. No doctor would tell *him* how to live! Bring on the greasy food!

Eventually, Mickey would pay for his recalcitrant demeanor and poor food choices. After consuming the "forbidden foods," he'd spend the better part of his weekend—day and night—sitting on the john. Others in the family learned of Mickey's predicament yet seldom expressed empathy. After all, in many respects, Mickey brought it all on himself when making poor dietary decisions.

A lot of his gastrointestinal distress was brought on by his consumption of stale, bacteria-developing coffee, which Mickey kept in a pot at room temperature, even in the heat of summer. He'd brew an entire pot and then let the pot sit for days, occasionally sipping cups of coffee until the pot went empty. The coffee probably grew mold spores by the hour, and Mickey refused to heed warnings from me and from others concerning the toxic brew.

Just imagine a steady diet of greasy food and bacteria-laden java—a recipe for anybody's bowel distress. The real mystery: Mickey would not modify his diet, even when he suffered from chronic diarrhea. Go figure.

Once, a gastroenterologist diagnosed Mickey as having celiac disease. I was actually relieved to discover this news. Alas, a diagnosis we could address with a reasonably attainable dietary modification! Alas, a series of medical and dietary changes we could initiate to help remedy the problem!

To clarify, celiac disease is an inflammation of the intestines in response to wheat products containing a substance known as gluten. Therefore, by eliminating wheat products and the irritating gluten substances, there could be a major relief at hand! No wheat, no intense bowel contractions! Alleluia!

I declared war on the celiac disease. I went on a shopping spree. There were countless gluten-free products in the supermarket to replace typical wheat products. I stocked up on gluten-free pasta, cookies, cereals, cakes, desserts, pizza—the works. It was a whole new start. The genesis of better health and happiness! And to ensure success of the new diet, I eliminated all wheat products from Mickey's kitchen, thwarting even the slightest temptation for Mickey to reach for a dreaded cupcake or other pain-causing wheat product.

A few weeks later, I discovered that, unbeknownst to me, Mickey had smuggled in "regular" cupcakes, breaded chicken, regular bread—all the things he was medically instructed to avoid in his new diet. Then, I heard his tale of woe, right from Mickey's lips, of how he had spent the previous three days in bathroom solitary confinement with chronic bowel distress. How he suffered, how he was in such gastrointestinal distress that all he could keep down was the mold-spore coffee that he reheated periodically until the stale coffee pot was consumed.

He knew better! Why did he sabotage himself that way? No matter how often I preached for an amendment of his diet, it was the same old self-destructive pattern of eating forbidden foods and eventually suffering the consequences.

I tried to empathize with Mickey regarding this irrational behavior. I even considered whether wheat products were tastier than the gluten-free substitutes, hence accounting for his noncompliance with the new diet regime. Then, my thoughts traveled deeper, wondering whether this dietary sabotaging was Mickey's twisted way of slowly committing suicide. (Going out with guns blazing, and bowels blazing, so why not eat the foods that taste better, though they are harmful?) The bottom line: Mickey would not tolerate anyone telling *him* what to eat or what not to eat. Nobody, but nobody, was about to command Mickey to change his eating habits!

After a while, a long while, I got tired of preaching about better dietary habits and simply resigned to the circumstances. My sister Rhonda, however, had more stamina than me and was relentless. She yelled at him to stop eating foods that were irritating his bowels. He became more stubborn. She yelled. He resisted. She yelled more. He resisted all the more. "A few cupcakes aren't going to do that much damage," he insisted.

Wanna bet?

Over time, I advised my sister to back off and to wait until our dad became hospitalized with chronic bowel distress and/or dehydration. "You can't change anybody else's thinking," I suggested. "All you can do is present options. If he wants to keep sabotaging himself, that's his choice," I bellowed. "He won't learn his lesson until he ends up in the hospital," I added in some prophetic statement of anger and frustration.

Sure enough, that is exactly what happened. Mickey ended up in the hospital with himself largely to blame as a consequence of living a life AMA (against medical advice). Hoisted by his own petard. Hanged by his own noose! Tripped by his own land mine! Tortured by his own stubborn refusal to make dietary modifications!

I could have strangled him when I met him in the emergency room after his 911 call. I remember entering the hospital and turning the corner as I advanced toward his emergency room gurney. From ten feet away, I could hear him proclaiming to the assessing nurse, "I have irritable bowel syndrome, you know. There's no cure for that."

By ignoring medical advice and eating anything he pleased, Mickey basically turned his back on well-intentioned medical professionals, family, and friends who encouraged him to make better food choices. I couldn't help but think, *Now you got exactly what you asked for, you stubborn ox. Is this the way you choose to live the rest of your life?*

Sadly, that hospitalization turned out to be much more than Mickey bargained for. The entire hospitalization, and subsequent recovery, would eventually lead to his endless string of defiant, resistant, and noncompliant behavior patterns accentuated by self-directed decisions AMA—and exactly his way or the highway!

The Downward Spiral and the Care Facility

After a three-week hospital stay to control chronic diarrhea, dehydration, and the onset of atrial fibrillation, a downward spiral and subsequent terminal decline began and continued for the span of almost two years. The initial discharge plan from the hospital involved Mickey's transfer to a skilled nursing facility, where Mickey's diet could be closely monitored, bowel accidents cleaned up twenty-four hours a day, medication carefully administered, and physical therapy initiated in response to leg-muscle atrophy caused by Mickey's three week, bedbound hospital stay.

Caring social workers now addressed issues that were previously brushed aside by Mickey in prior years (when my sister and I pleaded with him to address his overall deteriorating condition). In addition, new prescription eyeglasses were recommended along with dire dental care for teeth that were not only abscessing but actually crumbling and falling out! Spirometer exercises were ordered to expand his lungs and Mickey actually quit smoking while hospitalized, never to pick up a cigarette again! This nicotine abstinence was truly a minor miracle for the former chain smoker. Prior to this, no one who knew Mickey could ever recall a time when there was not a cigarette in his hand or mouth. In fact, every family photograph of Mickey reveals this truth. He was never, ever without a cigarette.

Meanwhile, dietitians carefully monitored healthy menus, psychologists asked probing questions, and urologists addressed bladder issues that were neglected for years subsequent to Mickey's earlier bouts with bladder cancer. A staff nun offered companionship and spiritual care. In short, all the king's horses and all the king's men (and women) tried to put Mickey back together again. The goal was to get Mickey back on his feet to the point of self-sufficiency and independent living once more.

On paper, this was a great care plan. However, the plan would only be effective if the patient decided to cooperate and follow the wisdom/advice of dedicated doctors and other health-care professionals.

Mickey refused to follow advice. He challenged all collective medical suggestions. Yes, all!

Just Leave Me Alone

Physical therapy sessions were declined by Mickey because he did not want to expend the effort, not even for "passive range-of-motion" therapy. This therapy involved a qualified therapist at the bedside simply moving legs and arms around while Mickey lay there, passively, without exertion on his part. Sure enough, as predicted by the physical therapist, Mickey's legs atrophied further because he refused to ambulate and rejected the therapist's attempts at passive therapy. Eventually, Mickey could not walk at all.

Prior to the ambulatory atrophy, Mickey insisted on keeping his urinary catheter inserted because he did not feel motivated to walk to the toilet (ten feet away) let alone use a commode or bedpan (two feet away). In Mickey's estimation, a catheter was so much easier and eliminated the need for regular toileting. However, Mickey was advised that prolonged dependence on a catheter could and would result in weak bladder control and/or urinary tract infections. But his response was "The catheter will stay in. I don't care what you say. I know what I want!" As predicted by the urologist, urinary tract infections eventually became a common occurrence in Mickey's life.

Mickey would only accept dental care if, and only if, the dentist would visit him in the facility. Then, dental care would only be accepted if tooth decay became so painful that extractions were the only course of action left to pursue.

Mickey was also advised to get hearing aids, but he felt that these were too inconvenient and bothersome. As a result, all visitors had to yell and scream at loud volumes so that Mickey could hear them. His common response to simple statements and inquiries became the repeated phrase "What? Speak louder! Why can't you just speak up?"

He refused to utilize a wireless audio headset I bought for him, which would enable TV viewing without blaring it at piercing volumes and disturbing other residents late at night. He also rejected a transistor radio–like amplifying device I presented to him in lieu of hearing aids. Floor staff and residents complained incessantly about the blaring television and about having to repeat phrases loudly in order to be heard and comprehended. Mickey's response was "Too bad. They should all speak louder. And if they don't like the volume of my TV, let them close *their* doors."

Over time, Mickey was "awarded" a private room at no extra charge. For the facility staff, it was easier than handling the constant complaints from roommates; and this way, the staff could close *Mickey's* door whenever the room's sound volume got out of hand. (I fantasized about having a T-shirt printed for Mickey with the words "Aggravate Others … Earn a Private Room!")

Along with refusing physical therapy, hearing aids, routine dental care, etc., Mickey refused eye exams, preferring to exist without glasses, and then complaining because the graphics on his TV were not large enough or that he couldn't read the newspaper because the print was too small.

Impossible to Live With

The downward spiraling continued over the course of time. Health aides were verbally abused by Mickey because pillows and bedspreads were not placed in the exact spots, plus or minus one inch of Mickey's preference. The visitor chairs in his room had to be positioned at precise, measureable angles in proximity to the bed or else Mickey would throw a temper tantrum. (Once, my sister spent at least ten minutes positioning and repositioning two chairs at Mickey's commands, and that episode resulted in another temper tantrum.)

Everything had to be Mickey's way or the highway!

The staff became increasingly agitated with Mickey's noncompliant, demanding, rigid demeanor.

A New Plan, a New Move

Eventually, I came up with a plan that would permit Mickey to live independently in an efficiency apartment. The plan involved Mickey's downsizing from his massive four-bedroom, seven-room apartment (now vacant because Mickey was residing in a care facility) to a one-bedroom efficiency designed for seniors. The plan also involved military veteran pension benefits to offset the cost of visiting health aides, visiting nurses, and other professionals. I offered to do the food shopping; Rhonda and the health aides would do the laundry and various errands. Voila!

The downsizing and furniture move took place just prior to Mickey's discharge from the care facility. This made practical sense, so Mickey could leave the facility and move right in to a clean, well-organized apartment stocked with food, supplies, and the works. The primary task at hand was to discard old furniture and old household goods from his former dwelling and keep only the necessities. After all, Mickey was downsizing from a dwelling that had seven rooms, bath, and storage cellar in favor of a one-bedroom efficiency apartment.

Oh, the pain! For years, Mickey was a hoarder. "Not the kind you see on those TV shows," Rhonda retorted. But it was close. Preparing to vacate Dad's original apartment was more difficult than cleaning up in the aftermath of an earthquake disaster. Among the vast inventory to address: fifteen empty orange juice bottles, washed out and waiting—just in case—and office supplies "borrowed" from previous employers (enough to equip a midsized Wall Street office complex). These included six staplers, three electric pencil sharpeners, at least ten thousand paper clips, and enough scrap paper to throw a ticker-tape parade the next time the Yankees won the Series. There were six broken umbrellas, three broken can openers, broken clocks and other broken appliances—all in storage, just in case they could ever be repaired. There were at least twenty-five cases of unopened soda cans, some of which had exploded in the intense heat during the previous summer; cans and cans of expired food; tons of sugar, mustard, and ketchup packets obtained over the years from fast food restaurants; at least one thousand rolls of toilet paper (yes, rolls!); about five hundred disposable razors; one-hundred fifty bars of soap, seventy-five cans of shaving cream (hey, they were on sale, so why not stock up?); and bed sheets stored from when George Washington slept there. And this is the grotesque part: there were bed bugs and other living creatures in his bedroom. I had to "bomb" the whole place with insecticide sprays before starting the cleanup invasion.

I attacked the apartment with a facemask, gloves, sturdy construction trash bags, and relentless prayers. I had my kids help take out the brown appliances. Furniture was donated to charity; clothes (dating back to the days of Abraham Lincoln) were dropped off at salvage bins, though I couldn't imagine who would want to wear that stuff, other than for Halloween. I hired a junk-removal company to take tons of unsalvageable junk away. It was hard work! Whatever wasn't discarded or transferred to the efficiency apartment was graciously stored by my sister at her home.

The New Digs

Eventually, Mickey left the care facility and moved into his beautiful, clean, fresh-smelling "downsized" apartment with all new nonbrown appliances. It was really nice. However, he proceeded to perseverate over all his possessions that were now missing. He crucified me for discarding all his "valuable" possessions that were lovingly hoarded at the other residence! In mid-July, he yelled, "Where are my winter boots, my winter hats ... my gloves?" (It was ninety-five degrees outside, honestly!) He grilled me endlessly about a missing pair of cufflinks. They were part of his costume jewelry collection that I never, ever saw him wear in his entire lifetime. (I never saw Dad in a pair of cufflinks. He never even had a shirt with the cuff holes required for the cufflinks. Yet he grieved heavily, over and over, about the lost cufflinks.) He hated me for my ruthless disposal of preciously hoarded "necessities."

To keep his new apartment uncluttered, my sister Rhonda volunteered her garage and most of her home as a storage facility for Mickey's undiscarded stuff. However, he could not bear the thought of being separated from his stuff, even though Rhonda lived only five miles away and promised to bring him whatever he needed, including the winter clothes in July, if it improved his mental health.

Rhonda eventually acquiesced to Mickey's demands and brought boxes and boxes of his possessions into that tiny apartment. He wasn't satisfied until the boxes were stacked high and tight, resembling a retail store warehouse just prior to a year-end closing sale!

The new plan was now in place. Utilizing the assistance of a daily visiting health aide, Mickey lived independently in this apartment for all of about three months. Mickey dismissed the visiting physical therapist because he did not want to put forth the effort that the therapist requested; he verbally abused the aide and she quit. He bribed another aide to smuggle in food products that did nothing but irritate his bowels and cause chronic diarrhea. He refused to socialize with friendly and well-meaning neighbors who lived in adjoining apartments. All that mattered to him was the nightly Yankees game on TV, viewed at ear-piercing volume ... but he couldn't even stay awake to watch the games most of the time.

Back to Another Care Facility

Soon, it was back to another care facility. The medical decline was attributed largely to Mickey's sabotaging of the home care plan. In short, Mickey refused to engage in any activity or endeavor that would have improved the overall quality of his life and daily functioning. His declining health now required twenty-four-hour skilled nursing attention at a nearby facility.

Once settled in to the new care facility, Mickey promptly criticized the dietitian, rejected any idea of physical therapy, and continued grieving over the missing cufflinks. His daily routine consisted of verbally abusing the facility staff, refusing to participate in any social activities, refusing to eat with anyone but himself, complaining that the TV volume wasn't loud enough even when it was turned on at maximum disturbing levels, insisting on wearing the catheter continuously, and generally criticizing everyone who tried to improve the quality of his life. He was the Grinch incarnate, and by comparison, he made Attila the Hun look like Snow White.

The Finish Line Gets Closer

It soon became apparent to everybody, including Mickey, that he was slowly dying. After all, how much could the body handle? Decades of cigarette smoke, a previous history of bowel cancer, bladder cancer, prostate cancer, irritable bowel syndrome, prior bowel resection surgery, celiac disease, macular degeneration, hearing loss, diminished mental capacity, tooth decay, painful osteoarthritis addressed with painkillers, chronic anxiety addressed with all kinds of antianxiety medications, bladder incontinence, and decreased ambulation, which resulted in a strict bedbound existence, all took its toll on him.

Mickey was miserable. But all offers made to improve the quality of his life were met with severe criticism and rejection. Often, he criticized the gifts (and the gift givers) who graced his presence. One night, in a moment of personal frustration, I commented to my sister, "No good deed goes unpunished" involving efforts to please the recalcitrant Mickey.

Mickey's world shrank down to a bed and four surrounding walls. His communication with the outside world dwindled down to the nightly televised Yankees game and occasional get-well cards from extended family members. His few friends no longer visited, most likely repulsed by the negative cloud that usually permeated the environment whenever Mickey launched into his familiar litany of complaints and criticisms.

A Few Bright Spots ... Not All Doom and Gloom

Though Dad was slowly deteriorating and dying, it wasn't all doom and gloom. Mickey still had his sense of humor and would share a joke or two during periods of momentary happiness.

Believe it or not, I also discovered a new spiritual connection with my father. When visiting alone with him, I would occasionally bring up the subject of religion and spirituality. He hated organized religion but often verbalized his belief in the presence of God and in salvation offered through the death and resurrection of Christ. (Not exactly his words, but you get the point.) One day, when Mickey was feeling very weak and lethargic, I summoned the courage at the end of the visit to invite him to pray with me. Though I am a pastor and frequently pray with others, this invitation was uncomfortable for me to extend. (I imagined it would be like a surgeon offering to operate on his/her own family member.) It simply felt awkward. But he agreed to the prayer!

We prayed for God's grace to come upon Mickey. I even threw in a petition for the forgiveness of sins. We both had tears in our eyes and we hugged at visit's end.

Prayer eventually became a regular ritual for us at the end of our private visits for quite some time. I felt good about this, because Mickey genuinely *wanted* to pray. He wasn't complying with my prayer requests simply to make me happy; and, after each prayer session, he would always follow the amen with "That was really nice. I feel better."

I remember walking away from our prayer visits and entering the facility elevator with a smile on my face—the dirty old man just prayed with me! I imagined famous conversion experiences detailed in the Bible: Zacchaeus, Matthew, Paul on the road to Damascus, the woman caught in adultery, and others. Well, add "Mickey in the facility" to that list of conversions! There was actually a spiritual side revealed to me, a side Mickey would never reveal to others.

There were other nonpainful visits too. We talked endlessly about the Yankees ... his first love. One day, Mickey came up with an idea: an all-Italian Yankees team comprised exclusively of great Italian American Yankees who played through the years, and what an impressive list it was: DiMaggio, Rizzuto, Berra, Martin, Crosetti, and the like. Mickey insisted that Lou Gehrig had Italian blood in his family tree! I laughed hysterically, but there was no arguing with him. "Gehrig was Italian. I am sure of it!" he shouted with eyes ablaze. I could not discern whether he was serious or joking.

Should We Take Him Home?

Though Mickey was medically failing beyond recovery, my sister and I would never dare to take Dad out of this facility and bring him to live in either of our homes. Primarily, because he would vehemently refuse to live with either of us, but most importantly, Rhonda and I each knew that a few months of twenty-four-hour contact with Dad under our roof would most likely result in homicide charges. One of us would eventually lose it psychologically and downright strangle him. (I add this comment sarcastically in a tongue-in-cheek way, but that explains how angry we often became in his presence.)

The Last Chapter

And so ... the recalcitrant, noncompliant, stubborn Mickey lived on at that care facility. There were the occasional cheerful visits, but mostly our visits had predictably negative tones. Mickey constantly complained about the food and his perceived mistreatment from the facility aides. (The facility aides were sick and tired of his demanding and demeaning comments. Some aides were chronically tired and worked double shifts. Can you blame them for being extremely irritated with Mickey at the end of a sixteen-hour day?) For the most part, Mickey was unlikeable and unlovable in the eyes of the staff, especially in those final days ... not at all like the personality of the former affable security guard who once flirted with the pretty bank tellers.

For a while, it seemed as if Mickey would live forever—in spite of the official medical observation, which was "failure to thrive." But then again, no mortal being on this planet lives forever. "Teach us to number our days," the Bible proclaims (Psalm 91:12).

Finally Called Home

It was a hot Sunday night, July 8, when Mickey died in his sleep at the facility. All alone but peaceful, just the way he wanted. No more doctors, no more therapists, no more specialists, dietitians, nurses, aides, or demanding adult children to tell him how he should live … or how he should die. He left the world *his way* and on *his terms,* even though all the king's horses and all the king's men (and women) once tried to put Mickey back together again.

I remember praying at his deathbed that night shortly after he expired. It was like praying over a concentration camp victim … how he had withered away to skin and bones. With tears in my eyes, I was overwhelmed with grief, anguish, fatigue, and an overall feeling that Mickey could have had a more comfortable final chapter in his life. But he refused "to live" those final days with any sense of meaning or purpose.

Later, after the body was picked up by the funeral director, my sister and I gathered Mickey's possessions and walked out of the facility into the dark summer night.

"He hated me," Rhonda sobbed in pain and anger.

"No!" I quickly replied. "He was so miserable he hated *everybody* and *everything!*"

What a sad ending.

During lighter moments, I now imagine what it might have been like at the moment of Mickey's death: his soul traveling heavenward on eagle's wings while he complained to the transporting divine eagle that there was a better way to get there. "Just let me drive! I know a better way!"

For the newspaper obituary photo, Rhonda and I selected Mickey's WWII navy portrait taken sometime after his eighteenth birthday. We didn't have the heart to post any current photos for the obituary because all recent pics would expose the recently cachectic, boney stature of a man who went from 175 pounds prior to the illness to a mere ninety-five pounds at death.

Mickey's funeral wishes were carried out just as he had indicated in writing years before. He actually preplanned his funeral to be complete with military honors including a flag-draped casket, sailors in full regalia, the playing of taps, and the works. Rhonda gave a heartfelt, sincere eulogy and we all honored Mickey at a postfuneral luncheon—at a New Jersey Italian restaurant, of course.

Recurring Themes

Notice the recurring spiritual themes in my father's story. Those prominent themes included the following:

- authority
- control
- guilt
- loss
- isolation
- anger
- grace

If you are preparing to say good-bye to your loved one, chances are high that these issues are also swirling about in your world. In the next chapter, I will offer some reflections on my personal experience along with some practical insights/suggestions for you to consider if you are preparing to address that final chapter of your aging parent's life.

Chapter 3

Preparing to Say Your Good-Byes: The Seven Spiritual Themes

I don't tell God how big my problems are ...
I tell my problems how big my God is.
—Author unknown

If you are "raising" your parents these days and/or spiritually preparing for their earthly departure, then perhaps you can relate to several of the issues and themes I have shared in the previous chapter when recounting my own experience with "My Way Mickey." Let's face it: your parents will continue aging with the passage of time. They will experience a myriad of changes, especially in those twilight years. Sometimes, the changes will necessitate sudden major adjustments for them and for you. At other times, developments will progress slowly or more methodically with each passing season. Either way, out of practical necessity, your parents may become more and more dependent on *you* for their medical, emotional, and spiritual well-being. Assuming your parents have not lost all cognition, here are some primary questions for you to ponder as you gaze into the future:

- How will you react to the changes and seasons of your aging parents' lives?
- How will you assist your parents if/when terminal illness rears its ugly head?

- How will you step forward to offer care and support for your elderly parents who may or may not value the ideas, suggestions, and options you offer for their improved well-being?
- How will you respect your parents' authority while balancing the conflicting ideologies that will most likely surface between you and them relative to end-of-life care?
- How will you contain your anger if your parents will not cooperate with sound medical advice?
- How will you trust in God and surrender to God's will?
- How will you draw upon the spiritual strength that God has already provided?
- How will you pray "thy will be done" and really mean it?

The following seven spiritual themes surfaced in my life as I prepared to say good-bye to my ailing father, and no doubt, they will manifest in your good-bye story as well:

- authority
- control
- guilt
- loss
- isolation
- anger
- grace

In this chapter, I will focus on each of these themes. The odds are high that you have similar issues, or will soon encounter them, in your relationship with your loved ones who are advancing toward the end of their lives.

1. Authority

One of the Ten Commandments is "Honor thy father and mother." The word "honor" is often interpreted as "respect." Those ancient Hebrews, who first received this directive from God via Moses, were well aware of the age-old advice "Respect your elders." Similarly, most of us are taught from an early age to respect the decisions, values, and ideologies of our parents. From birth to young adulthood, we are taught to value and honor the authoritative role of our parents, and this parental role seems to be built right in to the "office" of parent as part of the normative order of creation.

There is truly an implicit understanding in most family systems whereby the parents are in charge, with subservient roles assigned to the children. However, when those same children reach middle age and witness the diminished physical and cognitive capacities of their parents, then the parent-child hierarchy magically reverses. Somehow, the children begin to take charge of major life decisions for the well-being of their parents. Although this role reversal can be a traumatic time for the entire family system, it is painfully stressful for the parents themselves.

A classic parent-child reversal occurs in some family systems when the parents can no longer safely operate a motor vehicle due to physical impairments, cognitive deficits, diminished reflex times, etc. Obviously, such decline can jeopardize the parents' well-being and place other innocent motorists at risk for a potentially fatal automobile accident. During these times, the adult children have the unenviable task of addressing safety issues with their parents and, depending on the severity of the issue, may have to physically take the car keys away from their elderly parents to assure their safety as well as the safety of other motorists. This can result in the advent of World War III if the issues are not handled sensitively and with mutual respect.

How ironic this parent-child reversal can become! Years ago, the parents may have judiciously withheld the family car keys from a budding adolescent, or those same parents may have confiscated the car keys from a teen as a form of grounding for inappropriate behaviors. However, with the passage of time, the same child who was once the grounded later becomes the "grounder" in the interests of the parents' personal safety and well-being.

The psychological dynamics can be enormously painful for the parents. In most family systems and across most cultures, the parents are at the top of the authoritative totem pole … until, one day, these same parents must acquiesce to well-intentioned children who judiciously withhold the car keys. This reversal can be especially traumatic for the parents, because such withholding of the keys is a symbolic reminder of other successive losses normally negotiated with aging: loss of independence, loss of authority and power, loss of mobility, loss of friends through death, etc.

Compounding emotional stress, the parents may continue to regard their children as *children* and not as responsible adult members of society. Recently, one of my hospice patients stated, "I have a son who is fifty-eight years old, but I still look at him as if he were a kid. After all, he will always be my child, not my peer or my associate." Taken to its logical conclusion, how difficult it must be for many parents to suddenly feel less powerful than their kids, with those same kids now calling the shots vis-à-vis decisions that will impact their future living arrangements, medical care, and other critical end-of-life parameters.

In my relationship with my father, I am sure there were several days when Dad resented my taking control of his end-of-life care. Thankfully, I didn't have the car key battle. One day, Dad willingly gave up the car keys after a potentially fatal incident involving a near miss of an oncoming vehicle. Dad could not find the brakes momentarily, and it scared the bejeevers out of him, to the point where he could not trust *himself* to safely navigate behind the wheel. However, there were other issues in which my father had to yield to my authority after he became physically frail and medically debilitated. I had to take charge of the finances, the living arrangements, and other matters while serving as his power of attorney, health-care proxy, etc.

This was all a bitter pill for Mickey to swallow. For years, he enjoyed the role of *capofamiglia* (Italian for "head of the family"), and in earlier years, he wielded ultimate power and control over the family system. There were times when all of us—my mother, sister, and I—were afraid of Mickey and his frequent explosive displays of anger whenever he asserted himself in the capofamiglia role. In fact, there were times, years ago, when Dad would stick out his chest and jokingly refer to himself as the "lord and master" of our household. This was all said in jest, but we all knew it was the truth. There was no challenging Dad for control or authority in his household. No wonder, later in life, he greatly resented my efforts and the attempts of well-meaning medical personnel who suggested he modify his life and make healthier decisions. Surely, Mickey thought, *Nobody tells me what to do! I am the chief and capofamiglia!*

Sadly, for Mickey, he eventually became too physically exhausted to maintain the capofamiglia role toward the end of his life; out of fatigue and practical necessity, he yielded to others who were more capable of managing his end-of-life care.

Your Family System

The parent/child role reversal may be a big issue in your family right now. If so, my heartfelt prayers are with you. There is no easy way to navigate these murky waters. My sincere advice is to find a professional advocate or a team of professionals who can gently address these issues with you and your parent(s). When discussions get tense or anxiety ridden, as they inevitably will, outside professionals, such as social workers, psychologists, physicians, gerontologists, elder law specialists, chaplains, and others, can gently broach the sensitive topics, thereby serving to moderate negotiations and take some of the heat off you. Be careful, however, so that your parents do not perceive you and others as "piling on" and forcing your will over theirs.

No doubt, you have encountered, or will encounter, certain hot-button issues that evoke strong feelings on either side of the negotiation table involving your parents' future. Issues will rise to the forefront, including driving privileges, financial management, residential guidelines, safety monitoring, medication management/distribution, and other critical areas normally revolving around your parents' "activities of daily living" (commonly known as ADLs in the health-care industry). It is best not to engage in a knock-down, drag-out fight to the finish when you are at loggerheads with elderly parents. Instead, consider the alternative strategy of enlisting the advocacy of the professionals just mentioned.

Choose your battles carefully. Some issues are best left untouched for a while in order to maintain the peace. After all, you *do* want to respect your parents' wishes as long as they are not harming themselves or others along the way.

Whatever the circumstances, be on the lookout. As I briefly mentioned earlier in this chapter, some end-of-life issues will surface suddenly and without prior warning ... all the more reason to go into this season of life with eyes wide open, and with arms extended, to give and receive supportive hugs throughout the journey.

Reinforce your loving concern for your parents, or else they will feel bullied and overpowered during these sensitive times. They may feel as if you are no longer attentive to their concerns. Your parents are at an age when they want to be heard and understood.

The following prayer expresses their growing need to share their thoughts with you and with others:

A Prayer for Those Growing Old

> Lord, thou knowest I am growing older.
> Keep me from becoming talkative and possessed with the idea
> that I must express myself on every subject.

Release me from the craving to straighten out
everyone's affairs.

Keep me from the recital of endless detail.
Give me wings to get to the point.

Seal my lips when I am inclined
to tell of my aches and pains.
They are increasing with the years
and my love for speaking of them
grows sweeter as time goes by.

Teach me the glorious lesson that
occasionally I may be wrong.
Make me thoughtful, but not nosey;
helpful, but not bossy.

With my vast store of wisdom and experience
it does seem a pity not to use it all.
But Thou knowest, O Lord, that
I still want a few friends at the end.
Amen

—Author unknown

2. Control

This issue dovetails closely with the parent/child reversal highlighted
in the previous section. Everybody starts wondering who is *really* in
charge in the family system. Who has the final say on critical end-
of-life decisions? And the ultimate questions are these:

- What if your parent is alert and oriented, independently
functioning fairly well, yet engaged in self-destructive
behavior patterns?

- How do you deal with a belligerent parent who refuses to engage in basic behaviors that will improve his/her overall quality of life? For example, how do you react to a parent who
  - refuses to take medication without being persuaded;
  - refuses to engage in needed physical therapy;
  - refuses to wear hearing aids;
  - refuses to eat healthy foods;
  - refuses greatly needed optical and dental care;
  - refuses to socialize with others; or
  - refuses to follow the sound advice of doctors and other health-care professionals?

You may recall, in the previous chapter of this book, I shared that *all of the above* surfaced with "My Way Mickey." It was downright painful to watch this guy self-destruct. Time and time again, Mickey refused to cooperate with the sound suggestions of qualified medical professionals. Back then, I continually wrestled with internal tension between respecting Mickey's right to direct his own health-care decisions (even if those decisions were inappropriate) versus the option of jumping in and stripping Mickey of all self-directive powers. I did not want to bully my father into accepting specific care structures, yet it was too painful to sit back and watch the train wreck unfold.

In a similar vein, parents of young children often lament over battles waged when kids don't want to eat their vegetables, don't want to go to Sunday school, or don't want to socialize with family members. So what happens later in life when adult children have *parents* who become strong-willed and defy anybody or anyone who merely *suggests* a healthier way to live? That happened to me … and it may happen to you. Be aware of these delicate and sensitive relational patterns when they begin to develop.

Boundaries and Codependency

Two other critical issues generally surface for elderly parents and their adult children: boundaries and codependency.

Here's how you can identify unhealthy boundary/codependency issues: Whenever a challenge presents itself ask, "Is this problem *my* problem, or is it my parents' problem?" If you have difficulty differentiating between your parents' problems and your own problems, then chances are there are no healthy boundaries in place. Similarly, if you discover yourself absorbing all your parents' stress, you are in trouble—because then there is no demarcation line separating your life from theirs.

Please understand I am not suggesting that you step back and depersonalize your relationship with your parents. However, I am advising against falling into the trap of getting sucked in to all the pain to the extent that *you* can no longer function whenever your parents become dysfunctional.

At the risk of being redundant, I need to drive this point home. Codependency exists when the adult child basically believes the following: my parents' problem is *my* problem, my parents' misery is *my* misery; or my parents' choices are *my* choices—painful as they may be at times.

The adult child is drowning in the waters of codependency if/when there is no differentiation between the parents' actions and the adult child's state of happiness or well-being. In other words, if and when the adult child's happiness quotient is a direct variable related to the choices made by the parent, then there is trouble on the horizon.

In any relationship, one person's inappropriate actions should never become the barometer for another person's emotional health. Otherwise, unhealthy codependency issues rule the day.

An extensive exploration of this topic is beyond the scope of this book. However, if this issue is a major stumbling block for you, I highly recommend that you consult two landmark works that address these circumstances in greater detail and from a Judeo-Christian spiritual perspective. Regarding boundary issues, read *Boundaries: When to Say Yes, How to Say No to Take Control of Your Life* by Henry Cloud and John Townsend.[5] Regarding codependency issues, read *Love Is a Choice: The Definitive Book on Letting Go of Unhealthy Relationships* by Robert Hemfelt, Paul Meier, and Frank Minirth.[6]

Boundary and codependency issues happen in several of life's arenas, not just in the parent-child dynamic mentioned here. For example, anyone who has had an addict in the family system knows that the "acting out" of the addict can wreak havoc on all members of the family constellation. The nonaddicts in the family system must then learn two basic principles: you can't fix the addict's problem for the addict himself/herself and you can't allow your happiness and your healthy functioning to be directly contingent upon the addict's destructive behaviors. In other words, there needs to be a healthy demarcation line between the healthy, functioning member of the family and the self-destructive member of the family who is creating the toxic environment. This is basic survival: one cannot allow another toxic individual to drag him or her down with the ship!

To reflect back on my relationship with my father Mickey, I realized early on that my father resisted most of my efforts to improve the quality of his life. Time and time again, I would introduce healthier options for Mickey, like physical therapy, hearing aids, opportunities for socializing, etc. Inevitably, my efforts were met with resistance, anger, lack of appreciation, and even disdain. As a result, I became increasingly frustrated that my goals, objectives, and actions were not producing successful outcomes. But here's the rub: they were *my* goals, actions, and objectives, which were not aligned with Mickey's preferences. I took it personally whenever my father rejected my offerings. In short, I felt rejected. I personalized everything, and that was a classic codependent reaction on my part. I fell right into the emotional booby-trap set for all naïve codependents! I allowed myself to absorb the painful consequences of my father's unhealthy decisions. His bad choices became my pain—a classic example of the dangers of codependency and diluted boundary setting.

In the face of my father's apparent noncompliance regarding healthier options, I then had to choose between one of two reactive strategies: (1) push back harder, challenge him even stronger with all my mental energy, and force my will upon him or (2) offer the life-enhancing options but then learn to live with the consequences of Mickey's rejections and resultant self-destructive behaviors. By the grace of God, I eventually settled in to the second option, but it nearly killed me emotionally to stand back and watch the consequences unfold! Yes, I chose to "stand down" (military term?) because my father was mentally competent enough to make his own health-care decisions (be they grossly inappropriate at times), and he had the right to refuse treatment options as well as other enhancements that were offered along the way. Plain and simple.

I can't say this was easy for me to handle. It wasn't! I loved my father and wanted him to be happy, to thrive again, and to experience a more rewarding quality of life! I wanted to assist him in accomplishing his very own bucket list so that he could find some semblance of satisfying closure before riding off into the sunset. I wanted Mickey to go out with guns blazing and in a flourish of trumpets while grabbing life by the tail and whipping it around for a while. But remember that's what I desired, and I learned repeatedly that my wishes were not *his* wishes; my dreams were not *his* dreams; my fantasies were not *his* reality. Frequently, my feelings of anger and frustration stemmed from my own codependent issues rising to the forefront. I wanted to jump in and make things all better again, to do everything my way; and repeatedly, my persistent efforts were thwarted by my father who consistently poked holes in the medical care plans and found fault with just about every care strategy presented to him.

In retrospect, I learned some painful lessons about my codependent ways, but over time, I eventually discovered how to set healthier boundaries and thus avoid getting sucked in to the whirlpool of anger, frustration, and feelings of rejection.

For me, learning this lesson came with a high emotional price tag. There were moments along that journey when I did, in fact, create blurred boundaries and I allowed my blatant codependencies to surface. There were several occasions when I became inappropriately angry at my father when he refused to cooperate with health-care options I perceived to be beneficial and in his best interests.

Your Potential Codependency

Perhaps your elderly parents are making inappropriate and/or unhealthy lifestyle decisions. Think of your gut reactions.

- Can you step back and not get destroyed by all this?
- Can you set healthy boundaries and then live comfortably within those parameters, even when your parents don't comply with your vision?
- Can you sleep at night despite your elderly parents' rejection of the life that you envisioned for them?
- Can you resist the urge to control and dominate your parents' lives, especially when it kills you to observe the potential train wreck that may ensue as a consequence of their unhealthy parental behaviors?

You will discover a recurring theme of control as being one of the central issues presented in this book. The basic premise is you cannot control everything that happens! Life does not always turn out the way you want it to. And to quote the famous Rolling Stones tune, "You can't always get what you want."[7]

However, there is a spiritual strategy that will prove highly effective: you can decide to turn it over to the Lord in prayer. God's shoulders are much broader than yours, and God's wisdom exceeds that of your own by infinite measures. Jesus once said, "Come to me all you who are weary and burdened, and I will give you rest" (Matthew 11:28). When your loved one is relatively out of control, then by all means invoke the wisdom and grace of the One who can turn situations around. Get on your knees and pray for wisdom, guidance, strength, fortitude, and peace. As stated in Philippians 4:7, "And the peace of God, which transcends all understanding, will guard your hearts and minds in Christ Jesus."

God's grace, combined with the wisdom of caring health-care professionals, can go a long way to ensure your spiritual well-being throughout these trying times. Pray that you do not dissolve healthy boundaries between you and your parents. Also, pray fervently that codependency does not drain you of all your vitality and creativity.

3. Guilt

This issue closely follows those two issues mentioned earlier: the parent/child reversal and the need for control. What about guilt? In most cultures, there's nothing quite like good old-fashioned guilt feelings that frequently serve as a barometer for personal engagement with parents. Society often stereotypes the traits of age-old Jewish guilt, Italian guilt, Catholic guilt, etc., complete with the underlying, endless list of "shoulds." Maybe these statements are familiar to you:

- I should telephone Mom every day.
- I should visit the nursing home daily.
- I should consult that new medical specialist to learn about a new therapy.
- I should be more patient when things don't go my way.
- I should pray more often.
- I should be more loyal to my parent.
- I should make more personal sacrifices to ensure my parent's well-being.

The list can be endless. The expectations can be incredibly unrealistic. Yet many of us insist on dwelling with these same nagging thoughts consistently and persistently. If your personal guilt quotient is relatively high, then you know exactly how difficult it is to let yourself off the hook! In fact, you may be much more critical of yourself than others are with you! There may be periods of time when you repeat the same cognitive mantra "I could have … I should have … I would have …" Or "If only I said this …" Or "If only I had done that." And so on.

When will you ever stop "shoulding" on yourself? I know firsthand the destructive nature of "shoulding." When my father was ill and refusing treatments, I used to lie awake at night wondering, *Have I done enough to relieve his pain? Am I visiting often enough? Perhaps I should try a different approach? What if I walk into his room with a different attitude? Would that help?*

Then the "shoulding" began. *Maybe I should try one more thing … or another thing … or another … I should be more understanding of his circumstances and his pain. I should be more patient. I should be more understanding. I should be more kind and forgiving. I should be an example of faith under fire, not out of control under pressure. I should, I should, I should!*

Now *that* is a sign of codependency—when you find yourself "shoulding" all over the place. The best remedy for "shoulding" is a downright acknowledgment that you are human, after all. It is an eye-opening acknowledgment that you cannot be all things to all people. You can't be the messiah in all circumstances. You can't bring unlimited energy and unlimited wisdom to every challenging circumstance. You can't be perfect in every way, so why do you strive toward that unattainable goal, day in and day out?

I particularly find meaning in the words that Lutherans have used in their confessional liturgy: "We confess that we have sinned against God in thought, word, and deed … by what we have done, and *by what we have left undone*" (italics mine).[8]

For most of us, the things left undone are those that drive us crazy: the phone call we didn't make, the letter we didn't write, the doctor we didn't consult, the house we didn't clean, the gift we didn't buy, and on and on. How difficult it is to daily confront our human imperfections. How painful it is to realize that we're continually falling short of the mark we set for ourselves. How impossible it is to live up to our own personal expectations when all we ever do is raise the bar to unattainable levels. And oh, how we beat ourselves up, even crucify ourselves if anything is left undone!

Again, I speak from personal experience here! When my father was ill, I would continually ask myself if I had done enough to address the situation. I wanted to leave no stone unturned. I wanted to leave no "life-enhancement option" unexplored. This involved a seemingly endless search for the perfect care facility, a seemingly endless process of interviewing home health aide agencies, and the seemingly endless engaging in other "essential" tasks in managing my father's care. I had little left in my energy tank for any other responsibilities. Yet others clamored for my time and attention.

At that time, I was serving as a chaplain of a fairly large hospice organization. In addition to that full-time ministry, I preached and led worship every Sunday as a substitute preacher throughout New Jersey. I successfully managed to attend all my kids' sporting events, maintained a fairly large property at home, and even served as an adjunct college instructor one evening a week. Of course, all those responsibilities kept me busy, yet I continually felt as though I should devote more and more time toward the management of my father's health care. I recall trying to manipulate my busy schedule to allow for tons of phone calls to be placed to health-care professionals and others, all in a constant and persistent endeavor to manage my father's health-care options.

There were countless days (yes, days) spent completing the necessary hand written forms and documents to secure Mickey's veteran pension benefits, which would assist with the cost of health aides, medication, and the like. The Veterans Administration was helpful, courteous, and friendly, yet the entire application process took the better part of nine months! They were continually asking for more substantiating documents, forms, and qualifying letters before pension payouts would begin.

Eventually, when Mickey's personal funds were depleted, there were the hours and hours spent gathering substantial documents and bank statements needed for the Medicaid application, not to mention time set aside for the personal face-to-face Medicaid interview requirement. The interview took place after submitting a stack of application paperwork measuring at least eight inches high!

While this was going on, I'd receive daily phone calls from facility nurses and social workers, usually to inform me of how unruly my father was behaving toward the staff. Some of the health-care professionals threatened to discharge Mickey from the facility if he continued to sabotage the plan of care, etc.

One time I received a phone call indicating that Mickey tried to grope one of the staff nurses. (I told you he was a dirty old man!) I'll never forget how embarrassed I was when attending a subsequent care conference at the facility involving the staff social worker who began, "We won't refer to your Dad as a predator, but nonetheless, we must address the recent sexual harassment issue." I could have dug a hole in the ground and crawled right in. I was mortified yet pretended to be calm and composed as the facility care team established future monitoring procedures to keep "groping Mickey" in check.

So back to the guilt part. After all I did to secure quality care arrangements for my dying father, I still felt guilty that I did not take him home to live with me. As mentioned in the previous chapter, to this day I remain convinced that having Mickey live under my roof would have caused extreme anxiety—for him and me—not to mention the strain on my marriage with that kind of twenty-four-hour tension at home. Yet I felt that somehow I was abandoning my father if he remained in a care facility and not in my home!

Weighing heavily in my decision *not* to have Dad in my home came my vision of attempting to clean up Dad's watery bowel movements. (And everybody in my family knows I have a very weak stomach. Once, I even had a nightmare involving my desperate attempt to clean up a fecal Niagara Falls while gagging and barfing all over the place.)

No, thank you. No messy cleanups for me. I'm not *that* codependent to enlist for martyrdom as well!

Your Situation

Now back to you. Your feelings of guilt may be justified, after all. Perhaps you are not doing enough to care for your ailing parents. Perhaps you checked out emotionally and physically on your parents and you are finding it hard to live with the residual guilt. Perhaps you just can't bring yourself to the "caring table" because your parents neglected you years ago and you now unconsciously see their current struggles as a cosmic payback for the sins of their past. Perhaps you are stifling anger in response to unresolved conflicts from yesteryear. Your head tells you to bury the hatchet and move on, but your heart won't let go of the anger. Perhaps all the anger you are currently feeling is morphing into unhealthy guilt for not empathizing with the plight of your aging parents.

Here's a checklist of questions to gauge your guilt barometer:

- Are you really neglecting your parents, or are you simply taking time out for yourself?
- Are you able to delegate care tasks to others, or are you the martyr who won't accept help even when it is graciously offered?
- Are you able to ask for help, or are you afraid of inconveniencing others with your requests?
- Are you angry with your parents and feel that it is not appropriate to feel this anger?

- Are you cynical and tired all the time and correspondingly feeling guilty for wanting to take a nap instead of visiting your parent(s)?
- Are you able to take a few days off and not dwell on the concerns of your ailing parent(s)?
- Are you able to take a few days off without feeling guilty about not being there for your parent?
- Are you losing sleep or experiencing a decreased appetite because you simply can't relax?
- Are you upset whenever your parents claim you visit too infrequently?

Whatever you do, get in touch with those feelings. Guilt can be a healthy barometer if/when your behaviors warrant such feelings. However, if you are truly doing the best you can, then guilt can also function as a self-destructive pattern that serves no useful purpose for you or for your loved ones.

By all means, don't be manipulated by others who try to evoke guilt feelings in you! For example, there is nothing more potentially destructive from an emotional standpoint than any circumstance when the parent uses the word *never*. "You *never* visit me anymore! You *never* call! You *never* spend time with me!" Beware of these absolute or extreme indictments from others that are not grounded in reality.

Some parents demand a level of involvement that the adult children can never satisfy. Don't get sucked in by needy parents who are continually dissatisfied with your level of involvement! You could hold their hand twenty-four hours a day in a genuine display of love and affection, yet they're still not content! That emotional torture will drive you bonkers in the long run.

4. Loss

This is an extremely relevant issue to explore during the final days of your parents' lives. Be aware of the multitude of losses you and your parents may experience as a result of typical end-of-life transitions.

The feeling of loss usually surfaces at a time when your parents' world begins to get smaller and smaller. It usually starts with a "downsizing" of living space, perhaps moving from a midsized house to a senior independent cottage, to an assisted living arrangement, to a high-rise senior apartment dwelling, etc. Your parents' daily living environment literally shrinks in size, and this downsizing demands the often painful adjustment of discarding possessions. After all, how can one transfer all the possessions that once occupied a home (which may have contained storage space, such as an attic and/or basement) into a one- or two-bedroom senior arrangement? You guessed it. It is impossible.

The ultimate challenge is to work with your parents to gently discard the possessions that simply won't fit into your parents' new, smaller digs. Easier said than done! This process of sorting and discarding has the potential of causing major emotional distress for your parents and for you. Suddenly, a tug-of-war exists between their wanting to hold on to every earthly possession and your eagerness to discard, to donate, or to sell their old stuff.

Discarding possessions, in one way or another, represents a major loss for all parties. No doubt, there will be oodles of sentimental items that represent years and years of memories and experiences. How about that third set of china, once used for the annual family Thanksgiving dinner? Or how about those seven rooms filled with trinkets, knick-knacks, and collectibles from the previous larger dwelling your parents once occupied? Or that coffee table that doubled as a changing table when your babies visited for the weekend? The list goes on and on. Memories are attached to the artifacts. How can anybody release these precious keepsakes?

You may recall my story in which my father downsized from a dwelling that had seven rooms and bath to a one-bedroom efficiency apartment. Subsequently, for the remainder of his days on earth, my father grieved and grieved over the loss of possessions experienced during the downsizing process. These possessions were meaningful to him, including, oddly, the inexpensive cufflinks he never wore, nor ever intended to wear.

I realize now, as you may have already discovered in your situation, that the emotional loss felt by your parents when discarding material possessions goes far deeper than simply letting go of things. The discarding represents yet another painful loss endured in conjunction with several other significant losses, such as these:

- the loss of long-time friends through death
- the loss of physical and cognitive vitality
- the loss of short-term memory and the inability to perform simple mathematical calculations
- the loss of appetite
- the loss of vision
- the loss of bowel or bladder control
- the loss of joint flexibility
- the loss of coordination
- the loss of family pets
- the loss of familiar surroundings, such as the "old town," now urbanized
- the loss of independence
- the loss of respect from the younger generation
- the loss of a once active social life

The final blow occurs with the loss of overall health. A senior's world may shrink down to the confines of a bed and a nearby commode. The same person who once thought, *The world is my oyster!* may now be thinking *How far is it to the commode?* The same parent who once visited the awe-inspiring Grand Canyon may now discover that peering out a window for a few moments becomes the highlight of the day. Successive losses truly take their toll, emotionally and spiritually.

As your parents negotiate their losses, be prepared to experience your own grief as well. When you accompany your parents into the twilight of their lives, you will experience several losses, including, but certainly not limited to

- the loss of *your* independence as you provide direct care, or as you frequently visit your parents at their place of residence
- the loss of free time, as hours and hours are consumed addressing your parents' doctor appointments, specialists, etc.
- the loss of the relationship you once had with your parents, as once-philosophical conversations may be reduced to discussions centering upon their immediate survival needs
- the loss of your social life, as you decline social engagements to attend to your parents' needs
- the loss of personal energy and vitality due to the draining nature of living up to multiple role assignments, including the roles of direct caregiver, health-care proxy, power of attorney, house cleaner, errand runner, laundress, etc.
- the loss of patience and understanding
- the loss of time spent with your immediate family in lieu of addressing the demands of your parents' lives

The manner in which you negotiate these losses depends on a variety of factors, most notably the skills you acquired or did not acquire when managing previous losses in your life. Psychologists indicate that life consists of one's repeated ability to address loss and to move through loss as one journeys from season to season. There exists an entire lifespan of losses, including losing that first pet during childhood, losing friends and the old neighborhood through relocation, losing your first love, losing classmates, losing jobs, and so on. Life truly consists of multiple losses, negotiated successfully or unsuccessfully, from cradle to grave.

Losing parents is one of those major, heavy-duty losses. If you are reading this book, you are probably bracing for the loss of one or both of your parents.

Several adults who have lost both parents describe the uncomfortable feeling of being an orphan forever. Most "orphans" will agree that the first Father's Day or that first Mother's Day without that significant parent can be a tearful experience.

Some who are reading this section may feel as though they've lost their parents even *prior* to their death. This commonly occurs in end-stage Alzheimer's situations in which the adult child observes merely a shell of the one who once filled the role of parent. How painful it is to be in the presence of a parent who stares blankly into space and is no longer able to identify his/her own family member. Others witness the steady, slow diminishing cognition of parents who eventually forget how to accomplish basic tasks like brushing teeth or shaving. In a very real sense, it feels as though the parent has been lost already as most attempts at verbal communication prove fruitless.

Recently, I spoke to a woman who faithfully visited her mother in a nursing home. The mother was suffering from end-stage Alzheimer's disease and could barely keep her eyes open. All verbal ability was lost. There were simply no verbal responses, even when asked a direct question. Just blank stares, if that. One day during a joint visit, the daughter turned to me with tears in her eyes and said, "They call this the long good-bye, this Alzheimer's disease. Now I know exactly what they mean by that."

Your Season for Saying Good-Bye

The writer of Ecclesiastes once proclaimed, "There is a time for everything and a season for every activity under heaven" (Ecclesiastes

3:1). As you prepare to say good-bye to your parents, you will experience a season known clinically as "anticipatory grief." Though it is labeled "anticipatory" (as in the future), it is actually a *present* reality. There are losses experienced in the present moment as grief is felt in anticipation of the final loss. The mere thought of saying good-bye to a dear loved one can be a traumatic experience, as you well know.

It is a season to seek spiritual comfort and consolation through prayer, through meditation, through solitary walks, etc. There is tremendous comfort in solitude, with the reassuring confidence that the Lord can get you through any challenge or circumstance.

As my father slowly decelerated toward death, I spent countless quiet moments of prayer and reflection in my Prayer Chair (More will be shared on that topic later in the chapter.) I tried to envision my world without Dad, and each day I asked God to grant me the strength to address that day—whenever it would arrive via God's timetable. I also found great spiritual health through physical exercise, which consisted of distance runs to blow off stress and release greatly needed endorphins. It was during those runs when I tried to prepare myself mentally for the solitude I would later experience after my dad passed away.

My favorite expression during times of impending loss or actual loss is this: "If the Lord gets you to it, the Lord will get you through it." It is appropriate to acknowledge a time when the Lord has ushered in a new season of loss in your life. And remember that, just as the Lord guided you through previous losses and transitions in your life, he'll lead you through this one as well. If you ever need a reminder of God's grace, just leaf through the pages of your Bible to discover the various times and places in which the Lord led his servants through their own challenging times. I personally draw inspiration from the words of Psalm 34:4, 15, and 19 NRSV.

> I sought the Lord, and he answered me;
> And delivered me from all my fears.

> The eyes of the Lord are on the righteous
> And his ears are open to their cry.
>
> Many are the afflictions of the righteous;
> But the Lord rescues them from them all.

Remember the Lord won't let you down in your time of loss and anticipatory grief. I recall the words of an anonymous Christian who once addressed God with "Lord, help me to remember that no problem is ever too large for you and me to handle together!"

Go ahead and share *your* problems with the One who can sustain you—no matter what may come your way. Take heart in the words of St. Paul. "I can do all things through Him who strengthens me" (Philippians 4:13 NRSV).

5. Isolation

Realized losses and anticipatory losses quite often lead to a sense of isolation. You may feel isolated because nobody else really understands your situation in life. Nobody else really knows how you feel from day to day, and it seems that nobody else can relate to the draining and emotionally painful journey of accompanying a parent or both parents toward end-of-life care. Sure, there are those at the office or at the supermarket who politely inquire about your aging parents, but then they move on with their busy lives and you're left wondering if "out of sight" means "out of mind." For instance, a caring friend might say, "You and your parents are in my prayers," but that same caring friend does not offer a lending hand or an opportunity for you to find respite from the rigors of your journey.

Recently, a woman shared that ever since she began caring for her elderly mother, most of her friends simply stopped calling and stopped visiting. "They went on with their busy lives," she said. "It felt as though my mother had a contagious disease and nobody wanted to get near her, or me. Maybe, it was because caring for Mom became the primary focus of my life and my friends were sick of hearing about it. Or maybe they just couldn't relate. Or maybe I just became boring after a while and no fun to be around. Whatever happened, they (friends) stayed away and stopped communicating with me. I feel so alone."

This is a sad testimony of the isolation that a lot of caregivers feel during the final chapter of their parents' lives. Not only do friends and associates stay away, the caregivers feel trapped with unlimited responsibilities and begin declining invitations. There is simply no time—or no available sitters. One woman shared with me recently, "I want to go out and have a social life, but who is going to stay and watch my mom? Do I hire a sitter? If so, can I find one who can change an adult's diapers or help get Mom in and out of bed? Sometimes, it's just easier to stay home with Mom and not worry about all the details and arrangements.

Another isolating case was when a man who was caring for his dad wanted to participate in a caregiver's support group but found it difficult to get a sitter for his dad. Thankfully, he enrolled his father in our hospice program, which offered caring volunteers and home health aides who attended to the father's needs while the adult son participated in the support group. "Otherwise, I'd really feel like I have no life and nobody else to talk to," stated the son. "It gets awfully lonely in this house when it's just me and Dad. I start talking to the walls. And they never answer back."

Perhaps you are starting to talk to the walls. You're not insane. You're just trying to cope with the loneliness and isolation. Perhaps you play the television or the radio all day long just for the "companionship," or perhaps the highlight of your day as a caregiver is when the UPS delivery person comes to your door with the latest med delivery. At least he or she is somebody you can chat with for a minute or two!

Whatever your situation, please be aware of the dangers of loneliness and isolation, which can easily morph into depression or despair. Don't wait until you're depressed or mentally fried before seeking support. Please consider talking to a qualified therapist, social worker, chaplain, etc. who can assist you in coping with your isolation. These professionals can also offer suggestions for reconnecting with the world.

The hospice where I serve recently initiated a "phone buddy" network. These are volunteer callers who pick up the phone just to brighten the day of a harried caregiver. What a truly wonderful ministry! Those who receive these caring phone calls have the opportunity for human interaction and for venting at a time when everybody else is passing by in a rush to continue on with their own busy lives. Phone buddies are there to say, "I'm thinking of you. How are you today?" A simple gesture like that can go a long way to help a tired, burned-out caregiver who needs a bit of encouragement.

Some local churches offer caring Stephen Ministers who are trained to visit and support the stressed of their community. Hopefully, you are part of a church family or other house of worship that offers this kind of support. Some churches offer volunteer caregivers who sit with the elderly while the adult children attend worship services. This is another way that the adult children can be spiritually fed while traversing through the wilderness of anticipatory grief.

When my father was ill and needy, I had a few trusting friends in whom I found tremendous support. They allowed me to vent frustrations when stress levels were teeming. My wife, Kathy, was also a saint and completely understanding on those nights when I didn't even report home for dinner until nine o'clock because I was busy visiting my dad or discussing arrangements with the nighttime shift at his care facility.

It is essential that you find a few people in your life who are trusting, caring, and can confide in during your time of loneliness. Talk to those who will love you and support you unconditionally. A supportive friend or counselor can make all the difference in the world for you as you cope with the changes surrounding your life. If you are uncomfortably isolated and do not know where to start regarding a support network, please consult your physician or clergy person. By all means, do not try to be a lone ranger. This is no time for rugged individualism.

One final note regarding isolation: please ask for assistance when you need it. In my hospice ministry, I have witnessed so many caregivers who try to do everything themselves and almost die trying! I have seen martyr types who are worried, stressed out, sleep deprived, and miserable, yet they will not accept appropriate respite opportunities even when relief options are lovingly presented.

This rugged individualism is madness. We human beings are crafted by our Creator to be in community with one another. It truly "takes a village" (to borrow a slogan from a not-too-distant political campaign), and no one is expected to be entirely self-sufficient. If you need biblical justification, just read the second chapter of the first book of the Bible. In the creation narrative, God looked upon Adam and declared, "It is not good for the man to be alone" (Genesis 2:18). Likewise, it is not right that *you* should be alone either! Caring for your aging parent or making care decisions for that parent can be one of the most stressful times in your life. Acknowledge your need for support, and take care of yourself!

Recently, someone gave me "The Caregiver's Promise" document. These words are right on target for overworked caregivers.

The Caregiver's Promise

- Promise to remember that you have a life of your own. Being a caregiver is one part of that life, but it's not the entirety of your life.
- Promise to remember that taking care of yourself is not the same as being selfish. Even if no one notices but you, promise yourself you will notice.
- Promise to take yourself to a movie now and then; promise to take a nap or sleep an extra hour when you can.

- Promise that you will pick up the phone and ask someone for help. When they agree, promise not to beat yourself up for accepting their offer.
- Promise to find some time for yourself each and every day, and hold that time sacred.
- Promise too to let yourself cry long and hard and loud if you need to.
- When anger and resentment rear their heads, promise to let yourself feel the feelings, and then find safe ways to channel the powerful energy they contain.
- Promise to remember that no task is insignificant.
- Let this be your promise to yourself: to choose love over fear, compassion over judgment, empathy over self-righteousness. Remember that to give is to live, and give first to yourself so that you can freely give to others.
- Even though you may be surrounded by illness or struggle or death, promise not to forget that you are still very much alive.
- Promise to remember what truly matters.
- Promise that no matter how much you give and how frustrated you may sometimes feel, that you will remember that you too are receiving something glorious in return.
- Promise to let yourself receive, and to be grateful.
- Promise to remember that life is a never-ending circle, and that sometimes we are the caring and sometimes we are the cared-for.
- Last but not least, promise that someday, when you need a caregiver, you will do everything in your power to find someone at least half as caring as you.

—Rachel Snyder[9]

6. Anger

Some of us were raised in "religious" households where any display of anger was strictly prohibited. The prevailing thought was that expressions of anger were sinful and were to be regarded as a pathetic lack of self-control. However, I respond this way: Even Jesus had moments of anger! He expressed anger at the moneychangers in the temple; He became angry with Pharisees and other hypocrites who were not "practicing what they preached." He even got angry at a fig tree! (Matthew 21:18–19). So if Jesus got angry once in a while, why do a lot of people feel they must go to extremes to either conceal or stifle their own anger?

Let's face it: a lot of adult children get angry when interacting with their parents, and the anger is rooted in frustration. There are differing ideologies from one generation to the next, differing philosophies, and the generation gap continues to exist between middle agers and their senior parents. Once, I witnessed one senior who grew increasingly tired of her adult son who kept "badgering" her (her words) to change her lifestyle. After a while, the woman, in an expression of sheer disgust and anger, bought a T-shirt bearing words that emphatically proclaimed, "Leave Me Alone!" Honestly, it was a black T-shirt with large white letters, and she wore it often. Her son got the message.

Anger can also be a major emotion felt by adult children who are trying to provide a better life for their aging parents. As you learned from my story, I became angry with my father on a daily basis.

- He refused caring people and caring resources that were presented for an overall improvement in the quality of his life.
- He refused to wear hearing aids as a courtesy to those around him who then had to shout and scream to be heard.
- He refused to acknowledge the kind gestures of those who tried to make his life more pleasant.

- He refused to consider most opinions and suggestions from others that were offered for his well-being.

Those are just the headlines. The list is endless, but I am sure you get the point. Perhaps you are growing increasingly angry with your parents for not cooperating. If so, try to dig a bit deeper into those feelings to discover the true origin of all that anger. Ask yourself *why* you are angry and then do some soul searching. You may be angry due to one or more of these factors:

- The situation is perceptively out of control in your estimation.
- You've always had a conflicting relationship with your parents, and now old, unresolved conflicts are surfacing again.
- You see your parents as stubborn and noncompliant.
- You insist on having things your way and get upset whenever anybody challenges your opinions.
- You resent the demands your parents are making on your life and you just want more time to live your own life.
- You are frustrated because care demands are coming from both sides (parents and your children) and you feel unfairly caught in the middle.
- You feel dumped on by your parents, who now expect you to clean up their messy junk and wade through generally useless items that were hoarded over the years.
- You feel your parents are becoming more and more self-centered and expect you to do things they should be handling themselves.
- You feel your parents are becoming needy and they often try to guilt you into responding to their every need.
- You feel angry at God that your loving parents have life-limiting illnesses and this is simply not just or right.

- You feel angry toward doctors and other health-care professionals for not diagnosing your parent's terminal illness early enough—before things got out of hand.

Unmet Expectations

Now that you have explored some of your hot-button anger issues, try to find a common denominator or a common thread that seems to trigger your anger. Believe it or not, most anger jolts are caused by your own unmet expectations. When your expectations are not met to your satisfaction, you get frustrated.

These unmet expectations prevail in so many of life's arenas. Think of these circumstances: You are driving down the road and an aggressive motorist cuts you off, nearly causing an accident. Immediately, you respond in anger because you *expect* other motorists to be courteous and law-abiding. Or you are having dinner at a fancy restaurant, the service is poor, and you get increasingly angry. Why? You *expect* better service from that fine establishment. Or you are waiting in line at a customer service window and someone else barges ahead to the front demanding immediate attention. You get fuming mad. It is because—you guessed it—you *expect* order and decency among others who are standing in line.

Most of our angry outbursts occur because someone, some organization, some institution, or some entity did not live up to personal expectations. The common response is to feel cheated, frustrated, and enraged.

I recall a story about a gentleman who was hospitalized for a few days and the dietitian approached the patient about the next day's food menu. The patient responded, "Well, for breakfast I want scrambled eggs that are hard, crusty, and cold. I want bacon that is dripping with grease. I want ice-cold, stale coffee and cream that is so old it is curdling. The toast must be hard and black."

The hospital dietitian responded in shock, "We can't serve that kind of food around here."

"Why not? That's what I got here for the past two days. I've grown to expect such fine cuisine!"

What Do *You* Expect?

Now apply this concept to your relationship with your mother or father, or to both of them as a couple. The odds are high that you get angry because they simply do not carry on according to your perceived expectations. You can fill in the blank. My parents are not _____ enough. Perhaps, they're not affectionate enough, they're not smart enough, they're not giving enough, they're not cooperating enough, etc.

Now think, *Who is setting the bar here? Who is establishing the measuring stick?* You are! Somewhere along the line, you created a fantasy-like picture of how your parents *should* conduct themselves, and when they don't fulfill your fantasy expectations, you naturally get angry.

When dealing with my father toward the end of his life, I became angry on a regular basis. I had this preconceived vision of how the elderly are *supposed* to approach the end of life, and my father was not living up to my unreasonable expectations! I wanted a fairy-tale ending. I wanted a larger-than-life closure experience. I wanted the Hollywood version of the TV show *Father Knows Best,*[10] where everybody is polite, well dressed, courteous, kind, and mannerly. (For those readers under the age of fifty, you probably do not have a clue regarding my previous TV program reference. *Father Knows Best* was a sitcom filmed in the sixties in which the characters were often too good to be true and conflicts, if there ever were such things, were resolved in thirty minutes or less. The show's characters would often utter terms like *swell, gee whiz, jeepers creepers,* and *my golly.* The father figure always wore a tie, even when lounging around at home, and of course, the mother always wore an apron, had perfect hair, and made the only perfect casseroles on the planet).

Okay, so I wanted a *Father Knows Best* final chapter to my own father's life. What I got was more like *Everybody Loves Raymond*,[11] only the characters were not funny. I was angry most of the time. I was disappointed by my father's often inconsiderate behavior patterns and lack of concern for others. Dad simply wasn't measuring up to *my* unrealistic expectations for graceful dying!

If you find yourself growing angrier as time marches on, then stand in front of a mirror and ask yourself direct questions. "Am I expecting too much here? Am I expecting too much from my ailing parents? From the doctors and nurses? From the staff at the care facility? From other siblings who never seem to pitch in? And, drum roll, am I expecting too much from myself?"

The key to survival and reduced anger lies in lowering expectations to realistic levels. In retrospect, I believe I failed miserably in this area with my dad. (Generally, I tend to expect too much of myself, and this was projected on to my dying father.) The feelings that surfaced in response to unmet expectations clearly came out as unresolved anger toward Dad.

Time to Lower Expectations

If you are in a similar predicament, the time to lower expectations is right now. The sooner, the better. It is never too early to find more grace in the current situation that may be fueling your anger. You can practice anger management by starting with realistic expectations. These realistic expectations will do wonders to stabilize your blood pressure and to calm those volatile nerves.

I often practiced anger management techniques whenever circumstances with my dad got out of hand. First, I would pray just before visiting my father. I prayed for patience, wisdom, and understanding. Then, when in the presence of my father, whenever he said something I regarded as hurtful or unkind, I'd catch my breath, silently count to ten, and recompose myself to prevent angry outbursts. I prayed on the way home, after visiting my father and after dealing with his negativity. On those long drives, I listened to a CD of calm, soothing music that a nurse friend of mine provided. I practiced breathing exercises to calm down. And by the grace of God, I got pretty adept at identifying, and managing my anger. With God's help, I actually transformed my thinking from anger and disgust to empathy and even pity.

Please do not misunderstand me: I wasn't always calm, cool, and composed with my father. But over time, I learned how to step back and view the wider picture. My father was miserable with his particular quality of life, and my job was to be understanding and empathic. I eventually learned to embrace my part of the bargain.

I wish I had discovered the poem (printed below) when dealing with my father. These words would have helped me tremendously in discovering a place in my heart for empathy and consideration. Notice the following is written from the first-person perspective of the elderly parent.

> Do not ask me to remember.
> Don't try to make me understand.
> Let me rest and know you're with me.
> Kiss my cheek and hold my hand.
>
> I'm confused beyond your concept.
> I am sad and sick and lost.
> All I know is that I need you
> To be with me at all cost.
>
> Do not lose your patience with me.
> Do not scold or curse or cry.

I can't help the way I'm acting,
Can't be different 'though I try.

Just remember that I need you,
That the best of me is gone.
Please don't fail to stand beside me,
Love me 'til my life is done.

—Author unknown

You *can* manage your anger! Prayer goes a long way. As St. Paul once aptly penned, "And the peace of God, which transcends all understanding, will guard your hearts and minds in Christ Jesus" (Philippians 4:7). I also recommend that you meditate on this direct quote from the lips of Jesus: "Peace I leave with you; my peace I give you" (John 14:27).

May that peace gently replace the turmoil you feel whenever anger begins to swell up inside you. Lighten up, lower your expectations, and keep praying for the grace of God to help you cope with your anger.

7. Grace

I deliberately chose the theme of grace to appear at the end of my theme listing.

Please read the following Scripture verses slowly, and perhaps aloud:

> "I will be with you always, even to the end of the age" (Matthew 28:20).
> "When you pass through the waters, I will be with you" (Isaiah 43:2).

"Even though I walk through the valley of the shadow of death, I will fear no evil; For you are with me" (Psalm 23:4).

"Peace I leave with you" (John 14:27).

Now, ask yourself what these Bible verses have in common. What is the overarching theme? The verses are all about the presence and providence of God—for you! These verses, and so many other Scripture passages, bring comfort to weary travelers on the roads of life and offer security to those feeling all alone during the challenges and tasks of caregiving. These verses are reminders that God never intended for you to tackle caregiving issues without grace and help from above. It's too difficult a task to be a lone ranger.

As a hospice chaplain for almost two decades, I have conversed with hundreds and hundreds of caregivers. I discovered that most caregivers feel all alone when caring for a terminally ill parent. Common phrases uttered from their lips include the following:

- "Nobody else really knows what I'm going through."
- "My siblings are useless. They never help out."
- "I feel so tired and alone."
- "I feel like God never listens to my prayers anymore."
- "I don't know what resources are out there to help my parent(s)."
- "I wake up each morning with little to look forward to, other than the same old stuff with my parent(s) and the same exhaustion that repeats day in and day out with little or no help from anybody else."
- "I actually feel guilty when I envision their death as a relief from this mess."
- "When will this ever end?"
- "When will I have the strength to enjoy life again?"
- "I said an angry prayer to God today."

These and other statements are commonly verbalized by caregivers who are on the verge of burnout and are not feeling connected with others. They are not networking with those who can provide support and relief. They are physically, emotionally, and spiritually worn down in their efforts to do what's right for their elderly parents.

The spouse of one of my hospice patients recently gave me the following list, which he received from the Alzheimer's Association:

Ten Signs of Caregiver Stress

1. **Denial** about the disease and its effects on the person who has been diagnosed. "I know Mom's going to get better."
2. **Anger** at the person with Alzheimer's or others that no effective treatments or cures currently exist and that people don't understand what's going on. "If he asks me that question one more time, I'll scream."
3. **Social Withdrawal** from friends and activities that once brought pleasure. "I don't care about getting together with the neighbors anymore."
4. **Anxiety** about facing another day and what the future holds. "What happens when he needs more care than I can provide?"
5. **Depression** begins to affect the ability to cope. "I don't care anymore."
6. **Exhaustion** makes it nearly impossible to complete necessary daily tasks. "I'm too tired for this."
7. **Sleeplessness** caused by a never-ending list of concerns. "What if she wanders out of the house or falls and hurts herself?"
8. **Irritability** leads to moodiness and triggers negative responses and reactions. "Leave me alone!"
9. **Lack of Concentration** makes it difficult to perform familiar tasks. "I was so busy; I forgot we had an appointment."

10. **Health Problems** begin to take their toll, both mentally and physically. "I can't remember the last time I felt good."[12]

Constantly remind yourself that the Lord provides grace and peace for the journey through life. Our primary task as children of God is to be receptive to this support! Especially the support we can receive from others whom God places in our path.

The Cross to Bear

One day, even Jesus needed support and assistance to carry the load that was thrust upon him. You may recall the Good Friday story when Jesus was carrying the cross to the place of his execution. Jesus was exhausted, beaten, and had very little energy left for the tortuous journey to Calvary's hill. One can imagine Jesus stumbling and falling under the weight of that heavy cross that day. Just then, a man named Simon, from Cyrene, actually walked with Jesus and carried the cross for the Lord (Matthew 27:32). This Cyrenian lifted the burden of the cross from the Lord's shoulders in an act of grace and love.

One can't help but make the strong theological connection: if Jesus needed help carrying his cross, then why do you think you can carry your own cross without assistance? Don't you need help lifting your cross too? Don't you need assistance when the burdens of life weigh heavily on your shoulders and you feel you can't take another step? Don't you need spiritual strength to carry on? Of course you do!

The Lord promises spiritual fortification and nourishment for your journey. I now repeat an encouraging phrase which I shared earlier in this book. "Whatever you face in life, if the Lord gets you to it, the Lord will get you through it!"

How true this is! Think of the men and women whose personal stories are shared in the Bible. Time and again, when the storms of adversity came at them, they found a way by the grace of God. They discovered the Lord's guiding hand gently leading and nurturing.

I often recall the familiar story of Moses and the Hebrews fleeing from the Egyptian army. The Egyptian soldiers were breathing down their backs, with murder and destruction in their minds. Moses saw only a dead-end ahead … nothing but treacherous water. The people of God were trapped with uncrossable waters ahead and life-threatening soldiers behind. Just imagine how the Hebrew people may have felt, contemplating their destruction either by sword or by drowning. Neither of the options was salvific. Yet just then, God commanded Moses to lift up his staff, and the waters of the sea were parted, allowing God's people to safely cross to the other side!

What's the moral of the Moses story? Whatever happens in life, when you feel trapped, God will help you find a way out. Faithfully stated, the litany is repeated. "If the Lord gets you to it, the Lord will get you through it." As he guided the ancient Hebrews safely through the danger, the Lord will guide *you* safely through your seemingly insurmountable difficulties.

Reflecting back on my experiences with my dying father, I don't know what I would have done without the strength and encouragement I found in Scripture readings and in prayer. In those days, I reminded myself that I was not alone. I prayed for God's grace and wisdom. I prayed for patience and understanding. I prayed for endurance and spiritual strength. I opened my heart and soul to the Lord, and the Lord never let me down! Just as he rescued and saved the Hebrews at the Red Sea, and just as he lifted the burdens of Jesus through Simon on that fateful day, the Lord lifted me and guided me "through it" and safely to the other side.

You may be at a point in your caregiver journey where you do not see an end in sight. Or if you do see a light at the end of the proverbial tunnel, you are convinced that the light is actually coming from an oncoming train! Yet I advise you to "trust in the Lord with all your might, and lean not on your own understanding" (Proverbs 3:5). Things will eventually work out for you.

Get in Your Prayer Chair

For years, since I was very young, I have claimed a special prayer spot for my private devotions. I call it my "Prayer Chair." The chair is situated in a peaceful part of the house and faces a window—so I can look out upon God's beautiful creation whenever I sit there. (Notice the proper-noun designation for the chair.) For years and years now, every morning I have begun my day in the Prayer Chair. It's a spiritual time involving just me, a cup of tea, a Bible, and the Creator of the universe. While in the Prayer Chair, I think about my problems, I meditate, I pray for others, I read Bible verses and daily devotionals, I jot down sermon ideas for an upcoming homily … But mostly, I just sit there and allow the Spirit of God to remind me that I'm never alone. I am reminded of God's ever-present support, which will be with me right "till the end of the age" (Matthew 28). I take comfort and solace in knowing that the Lord of creation cares enough about me to join me each day as I share my life's concerns. While in the Prayer Chair, I know that none of my concerns are ever too big or too small for God's attention.

Of course, I pray several times throughout any given day, but there's nothing quite like starting the day in that Prayer Chair. When I'm on vacation or in some hotel room far away from home, I find a chair that I can designate as a Prayer Chair for the day, and I'm spiritually connected, right on the spot. (By the way, I often see hotel rooms that have printed cards on the nightstand to announce that the room is connected with a high-speed Internet feature. I'm tempted to leave a note on the bedside chair of the hotel room indicating for the next traveler that the chair has a high-speed spiritual connection to God! And no external modems or routers are necessary. Just sit in the Prayer Chair and instantly experience a twenty-four-hour high-speed connection to the heavenly server!)

I highly encourage you to designate a Prayer Chair of your own. But whatever you do, when you sit in your Prayer Chair, don't get uptight about the exact words, phrases, or even the agenda relative to your connection time with God. Just sit and think. Dedicate your thoughts, your concerns, your joys, your challenges, and whatever comes to mind to the God who knows you better than you know yourself. (See Psalm 139:1–5.) As time goes by, you will discover the Prayer Chair time to be the best possible investment you can make for your overall well-being.

Above all, when you sit in your Prayer Chair, remind yourself that you are never alone and that the omnipotent God of the universe will send grace and peace upon your challenging circumstances. Don't be surprised if, over time, you begin to discover more mental, emotional, and spiritual energy coursing through your veins because of time spent in your Prayer Chair.

The words of St. Paul encapsulate my hope for you.

> I pray that out of his glorious riches he may strengthen you with power through his Spirit in your inner being, so that Christ may dwell in your hearts through faith. And I pray that you, being rooted and established in love, may have the power, together with all the saints, to grasp how wide and long and high and deep is the love of Christ, and to know this love that surpasses knowledge—that you may be filled to the measure of all the fullness of God.
>
> Now to him who is able to do immeasurably more than all we ask or imagine, according to his power that is at work with us, to him be the glory in the church and in Christ Jesus throughout all generations, forever and ever! Amen.
>
> —Ephesians 3:16–21

Chapter 4

Mom: "Betty Boop"

In my anguish I cried to the Lord, and he answered by setting me
free. I was pushed back and about to fall, but the Lord helped me.
—Psalm 118:5, 13

You have already read my story of preparing to say good-bye to
my father ("My Way Mickey," chapter 2). Well, believe it or not,
as if some divine synchronicity were at work, my mother began a
downward spiral during the same period of time. My sister and I
had the whirlwind experience of addressing the care needs of each
of our parents simultaneously, which made for a terrific juggling act
of doctor appointments, telephone calls, voice-mail messages, and
various pep talks to encourage our parents to live their lives to the
fullest. Mom's story follows.

The Indefatigable Betty Boop

My mother, Betty, was affectionately nicknamed Betty Boop by
several of her lifelong friends. She could have easily been labeled
Bubbling Betty. My earliest childhood memories paint a picture of a
woman who had the industrial nature and productivity of an entire
cleaning crew. Betty was a stay-at-home mom who had a compulsive-
like demeanor regarding housework. She was the window-washing
type (all the time). She cleaned everything constantly and particularly

declared war on soiled laundry, which I provided in abundance during my childhood years.

Betty was truly the laundry queen. My sister and I had the cleanest clothes on the block. I remember my little league baseball uniforms, which were immaculately sanitized to the point of embarrassment. It looked like I never left the laundry room! Other kids had the usual grass stains on their knees along with brown slide marks on the backs of their baseball uniforms from sliding into home plate. Not me. I slid just as much as they did. I tumbled after fly balls just as often as my teammates. Yet I had this sparkling clean uniform unmatched by anyone else in town. I could have posed for a bleach commercial. Once, I remember listening to my pastor's sermon about the transfigured robes of Jesus (being white as light), but in my mind, I knew Mom could give Jesus a run for his money in the laundry department.

And here's the kicker: Betty was the laundry queen and never had a state-of-the-art washing machine. We were so poor we had an old washing machine in the kitchen that had to be tethered to the kitchen sink whenever the rinse cycle began.

And a dryer? Forget about it. There was no dryer. Either Mom ran a clothesline outside or she carried wet clothes down the block to the coin-operated laundry mat for quick drying (in the winter months, when hanging clothes outside would freeze them).

Betty did it all: cooking, cleaning, ironing, shopping, banking, paying bills, repairing small appliances around the house, painting the walls, polishing furniture and waxing the wooden staircases, vacuuming and sweeping, cleaning up after the dog, breaking up fights between my sister and me, helping with homework, attending all my sporting events, hosting family holiday meals, shopping and wrapping for Christmas, tree trimming, and the works! I never saw her take a nap in those early years. In fact, she never sat down until after dinner, and after washing and drying the dishes, and after preparing lunches for all of us to take the next day, and after returning phone calls to her sister Florence. Then, when she did eventually sit down and begin to watch television, my dad would ask for a cup of coffee, and up she sprang like a jack-in-the-box.

Years and years of this activity, however, began to take its toll. It was hard work, and Betty grew tired of being verbally bullied and criticized by her husband, Mickey. The harder she worked, the more orders and demands would come down from Mickey. It was like she was the hired maid, or worse, an indentured servant. What a thankless job it was for her.

My parents had a functional marriage only, with no outward displays of love or affection between them. No exchanges of cards or gifts for birthdays, anniversaries, or holidays. No outward embraces. No "I love you" expressions, verbal or nonverbal. No treats to a restaurant or to a diner so that Betty might get a night off from the constant manual labor.

Meals were cooked in an oven that should have been pronounced "dead," complete with its door falling off the hinges—all the while needing to be propped shut with a kitchen chair. Betty hated cooking, and she was a primitive cook to say the least. Most mealtimes were graced by us poking fun at the lousy food while Mom tried to laugh it off. (In the words of Rodney Dangerfield, "The food was so bad we prayed *after* the meals.") We were sometimes cruel with our food critiques, while Betty half-jokingly invited us to eat at the neighbors' homes if we weren't satisfied. Most nights, that invitation was actually an attractive proposal. It was not uncommon for all of us to break open the peanut butter and jelly jars shortly after a typically disastrous meal.

Betty was a loving soul and a terrific mother. Just not a gourmet chef by any means!

Tension All Around

Betty played a subservient role during that marriage and hated it. Arguments filled the air most nights. During the summer, all windows were open because only "rich people" had air-conditioning.

With the windows open, neighbors on either side could hear the blow-by-blow debates and heated discussions between Mickey and Betty. The other neighbors fought with their windows wide open as well. Needless to say, there were few family secrets among neighbors, since they lived just a few feet from one another.

My parents weren't the only couple to "air their dirty laundry." Everybody's parents were conflicted in that poverty-stricken blue-collar neighborhood. One night somebody's Dad got drunk and angry and proceeded to walk down the alley with a pistol intending to shoot his wife. Another night, we learned that somebody else's dad committed suicide by hanging himself in the closet with a belt. (We all heard the blood-curdling screams from his daughter who walked into the house that afternoon, opened the closet door, and discovered the horrific scene.)

It wasn't a pretty neighborhood as everybody was poor, frustrated, and at wit's end, especially during the sweltering hot summers. And there was the occasional racial tension in the neighborhood. Kids would be in the middle of a sandlot game and the name-calling would break out. "Nigger!" "Wop!" "Mick!" And the next thing you know, fists would start flying. It was a regular thing, this openly expressed hostility and rage. Summer heat always brought out the worst in behaviors and demeanors.

The Declaration of Independence

Inside our house, anger and tension were constant companions. The yelling and shouting persisted for almost forty years, until Betty finally found the nerve to break loose from her domestic bondage. After years of biding her time, patiently waiting for my sister and me to grow up and find places of our own, Betty made her move. Unannounced, when my dad was away at work, Betty enlisted the help of some neighbors and family members and secretly vacated the dwelling, taking with her a few pieces of furniture in addition to half of the money that was in their miniscule joint checking account.

I wasn't there during the move because I was away at graduate school. But I learned later that my father came home from work that day to find some furniture missing, lights out, and a "Dear John" letter on the table from his angry wife announcing her intention to file for divorce. And file she did! Betty took up residence in a local senior housing complex and landed a job as a switchboard operator at the community hospital. (She had been a switchboard operator prior to marriage, so why not use that acquired experience in a new job?) Betty declared her independence! She was no longer an indentured servant in a cold, functional marriage arrangement.

The judge's gavel finalized the divorce just one day prior to their fortieth wedding anniversary.

The Mental Health Issue

In earlier years, way before the divorce, Betty Boop was known as the life of the party. Her bubbly, effervescent personality was a delight to everyone. She loved to clown around at parties while putting on outrageous hats for gags. She sang songs and told the same jokes at holiday gatherings until we were in stitches. She danced on the diving board of her friend Lucille's pool, faking a strip-tease number with a beach towel. What a fun-loving gal! It was truly remarkable that Betty could be so cheerful, while coping daily with the heartbreak of a dysfunctional, unaffectionate marital life.

Over time, however, something had to give. Eventually, depression reared its ugly head. Part of the depression was no doubt attributed to an inherited genetic construction. There was a long history of depression that ran on Betty's side of the family. However, a major contributing factor to the depression was the overall feeling of despair having been trapped in a terrible marriage for all those years. Decades of marital misery was bound to take its toll emotionally.

In this case, the symptoms of distress became manifest in the form of chronic depression.

The depression symptoms surfaced intermittently throughout the years preceding the marital separation but would later peak and plague Betty for the rest of her life.

Once, when still married to Mickey, the depression was so intense that Betty was admitted to the behavioral health wing of the local hospital. While Betty was hospitalized, Mickey claimed that Betty was not really sick at all, just attention starved. In an interview with the hospital psychiatrist, Mickey indicated that the best therapy for Betty was for her to go back home and resume her "duties." (Translation: Mickey wanted his servant back in the house again. After all, warming up TV dinners was beginning to get old for him.)

Betty was eventually discharged from her behavioral health intervention in the hospital, and with a fresh prescription for Zoloft, she jumped right back into the indentured servant role.

The years marched on, the depression spells came and went, and certain cyclical patterns began to surface. Betty's depression spells predictably spun out of control in late fall and reached their peak just before Christmas. It was a typical "seasonal affective disorder." My sister and I would cope by adding dry, sarcastic humor indicating that whenever Christmas trees appeared in the store windows, it would be *that* time again: time to watch Mom wilt and flop like a rag doll.

During those depressions, there was no cheering her, and no motivational pep talks could encourage her or lift her out of that funk. She refused to talk to a psychotherapist but did eventually consent to regular consultations with a psychiatrist who monitored her meds on a quarterly basis. The meds never seemed to remedy the depression and Betty became adept at play-acting during routine psychiatric follow-up visits. She could be totally depressed during her psychiatrist appointments yet convince the psychiatrist that all was fine. Just renew the prescriptions, and move on. This charade would linger for the better part of two or three years until the next emotional crash and its resultant inpatient treatment period. The repetitive depression cycle grew worse with time.

Lethargy and Listlessness

The years marched on. The mood cycles came and went. Eventually, Betty became lethargic and listless on a regular basis, not just in a cyclical pattern. She would attend holiday gatherings and fall asleep in a room full of loud people. She had this flat affect constantly and had an annoying habit of saying "What?" after each verbal cue. It wasn't that she was hard of hearing. She simply needed time to process even tiny bits of information.

"Betty, do you want sugar for your coffee?"

"What?"

"Sugar for your coffee?"

"What? Yeah, I guess."

"Merry Christmas, Betty."

"What?"

During that time in her life, Betty was noticeably and outwardly depressed. She was in this neutral funk with a flat affect and nonenergized demeanor sometimes resembling mild catatonia. Whenever she did manufacture a smile, it seemed forced and unnatural. Those around Betty began to notice a proliferation of wrinkles branching throughout her forehead and temporal regions, precipitated by all the emotional pain she carried through the years.

Rhonda tried earnestly to get Betty to socialize with others in the hopes that interpersonal interaction would cheer her up. Rhonda, a lifelong dog handler, breeder, and groomer, frequently took Betty to the weekend dog shows, but Betty oftentimes ended up sleeping in the car or appeared disinterested in the events of the day. There seemed to be no way to snap Betty out of the blue funk and melancholy demeanor.

But then, for a season, things began to change.

Bubbling Betty

Once, after months and months of feeling depressed, Betty suddenly perked up, became happier and more invigorated, and remained bubbly for about a month or two. There was no curbing her enthusiastic nature! She was ecstatic! She was happy! She smiled often!

During those up times, she talked incessantly and sometimes laughed uncontrollably. She found happiness again and went on shopping sprees, purchasing items she didn't need with money she didn't have (thanks to the wonder of credit cards). She discovered an unlimited energy that only needed to be fed with two hours of sleep each night. Bubbling with newfound energy, late night phone calls to unsuspecting friends and family members now became the norm.

Most nights, Betty found herself still pumped up at three o'clock in the morning and attentive to every item up for bid on the home shopping TV channel. She purchased gifts for everybody. She couldn't stop watching and buying, watching and buying ... She could not resist a sale—any sale.

Now, the whole world looked wonderful to Betty Boop. The all-night TV shopping channel became the conduit through which Betty purchased hundreds of jewelry items and clothing. She racked up thousands and thousands of dollars worth of credit charges with absolutely no plan for paying off the debt. (Estimating conservatively, accounting for Betty's meager switchboard pay, social security income, and monthly living expenses, it would have taken over fifty years to pay off all those credit cards, and Betty could not have cared less!)

After discovering the excessive spending patterns, my sister and I had to step in, be the bad guys, and stop the spending rampage. In short, we had to apply a tourniquet to stop the financial bleeding. We demonstrated to Betty the impossibility of paying for all the stuff she acquired, and then we returned most of the jewelry, obtaining thousands of dollars in refunds, much to the chagrin of Betty Boop.

The ironic twist was that Betty *never* wore the jewelry she purchased, *never* wore the clothes she bought on credit, and almost all of the items she obtained during the spending sprees remained boxed and stashed away in her closets. Many of the boxes were never even opened or their contents examined.

Apparently, Betty enjoyed the thrill of spending money. Period. The hunt was more exciting than the reward.

Rhonda and I were curious as to why Betty was so unusually hyper and bubbly all the time, especially in the aftermath of the typical, lengthy depression spells. It didn't take long for the psychiatrist to diagnose Betty as having bipolar disorder, a mood-swing condition manifested by alternating periods of debilitating depression and hyper mania. The diagnosis called for more psychotropic meds and led to more unpredictable fun for the entire family. If left unmedicated, Betty might have spells of depression—or mania—for weeks and months at a time. Therefore, my sister and I had to closely monitor Betty's medication in an effort to keep her on even keel.

The Fight for Independence, the Struggle with Inertia

Betty insisted on living alone, in her one-bedroom senior citizen apartment, even though Rhonda and I encouraged her to stay at our homes periodically. She lived independently well into her early eighties, but the octogenarian decade would not be a graceful one for Betty. Throughout the constant psychiatric tug-of-war that existed in her mind between depression and euphoria, it was the depression that became the stronger force.

The lethargy and inertia began to take its toll, fueled by the chronic impact of her depression. Over that time period, Betty became extremely lethargic, lost her appetite, had no interest in socializing, could not keep track of her meds, and began to neglect personal hygiene.

Years before, Betty was a real wiz at balancing her personal checkbook. Now, that same checkbook contained scribbles, mathematical corrections, cross-outs, and microscopic notations that were indecipherable to anyone but her.

The depression was relentless, and Betty was losing the battle. Just the thought of taking the elevator to the building's lobby to retrieve daily mail was like considering an expedition to the core of the earth.

Rhonda and I invited Betty to socialize. Her answer was consistently and predictably in the negative.

"Mom, how about a trip to the beauty salon?"

"What? No. I'm not going."

"How about a trip to the ice cream parlor?"

"What? No."

"Mom, your teeth are decaying. You need urgent dental care."

"What? No way."

"How do you feel?"

"What? I dunno."

Betty's days consisted of sitting in a recliner chair and watching television twenty hours a day. The channel was locked on the Animal Planet station. She resumed her cigarette smoking habit, after having quit for several years.

She did not feel like preparing meals, so Rhonda and I obtained fresh fruits and microwavable instant dinners, but Betty was too disinterested to bother and had no appetite anyway. Her sister Florence, now in her nineties, lived just two doors away and brought over home cooked meals and soups, yet Betty had no interest in the food. She got weaker and weaker, and in spite of several warnings about leg muscle atrophy, Betty refused to walk any farther than the distance between the recliner and the bathroom. Betty became reclusive. It was all so hard to fathom. Betty Boop, once the life of every party, now isolated, wrinkled, emaciated, and listless.

Time for a Change

After repeated invitations to live with me and my family for a while, and Betty's repeated resistance to those invites, Rhonda and I developed a compromise plan as a last-ditch effort for our mother to maintain her independent living arrangement. We decided our mother could live independently as long as the following happened:

a.   She allowed me to fill pillboxes and monitor her weekly meds.

b.   She received Meals on Wheels, which is a community nutritional program delivering hot and cold meals daily.

c.   She made some effort to live a life, keep medical appointments, and exist as a human being in a world that was broader than the confines of her recliner (where she preferred to vegetate and chain-smoke).

Betty agreed to the terms.

In addition, the plan called for Rhonda and me to do routine grocery shopping while Betty's sister Florence volunteered to assist with the laundry and mail collections.

This compromise plan worked for the better part of a year, but in retrospect, we were all simply enabling Betty to just sit around, remain isolated, and smoke cigarettes. On trips to fill Betty's pillboxes, I noticed that some days Betty was too lethargic to take her meds, which were now separated into daily pillbox installments. There were sixteen different pills to be consumed each day to combat depression, hypertension, anxiety, bladder incontinence, osteoporosis, an iron deficiency, and joint pain.

Betty could not concentrate on simple subject matters, stared aimlessly at the television, lost interest in opening her mail, and became weaker and weaker to the point of nearly losing all ambulatory functioning.

Pep talks did not seem to change Betty's state of lethargy. Medication did not seem to make a difference, nor did visitations, holiday gatherings, or anything else. She lost interest in everything and would occasionally state, "Sometimes, I just wish I could fall asleep and never wake up."

A Crisis and the Aftermath

One night, I received a distress call from Aunt Florence that Betty was especially despondent and had lower leg edema. It was off to the emergency room and the advent of a hospital stay that revealed some cardiac abnormalities, dehydration, and cognitive deficits. Betty could not live alone in this condition, so the hospital discharge plan called for Betty to stay at a rehab unit for physical therapy, medication monitoring, and socialization—all in an effort to bring a bit of new life to her listless existence.

Upon discharge from the hospital, Betty was "temporarily" assigned to a rehab unit designed for the demented; it was the only available bed in the facility. There was an understanding that Betty would be transferred to a "happier" floor once another room became available in the "normal" rehab wing of the facility.

Well, the dementia unit was another nightmare. Instead of brightening Betty's spirits, it became another downer.

Mealtimes were shared with catatonic and/or demented residents. Some of the "energized" Alzheimer's residents often resorted to either stealing other's food or throwing the food around the room with very little supervision coming from the resident staff. And Betty, already in a weakened condition topped off by chronic depression, simply sat there staring off into space. It was a blessing that she received daily visits from her family, or Betty would have sunk even deeper into a lifeless funk in that gloomy environment.

Physical therapy sessions became relatively ineffective, because the facility policy called for Betty to remain wheelchair bound for the entire day (other than during those brief therapy times). The facility staff indicated that the wheelchair rule was a precaution against potential falls. This may have been true, but it became apparent over time that the wheelchair rule was a facility safeguard to avoid potential lawsuits should an unattended resident take a header whenever the fun-loving staff was clowning around at the nurse's station.

The Quandary

I had to get my mother out of this depressing facility. However, she was in no condition to live alone and was not independent enough to function in an assisted living environment. Furthermore, for personal safety and medical reasons, Betty could not be left alone during the day at either my house or my sister's house when we were away at our jobs. Hiring a private aide was financially prohibitive.

So what now?

I proposed a plan whereby Betty could resume living in her apartment and attend adult day care during the week. The county offered to pay the entire tab, which included transportation, meals, medication management, socialization, arts and crafts, holiday parties ... the works. When I introduced Betty to the facility with the intention to have a "look around" for consideration, she begged and pleaded with me not to enroll her in the program. With tears in her eyes, she refused to enroll, and the last thing I wanted to do was to force her to participate.

So what now?

Well, by the grace of God, a county social worker suggested that Betty be placed in a Christian care facility in which she could live fairly independently (her own apartment!) along with greater nursing supervision than would be provided in a typical assisted living environment. The facility would provide all meals, along with physical therapy, daily social activities including worship services, and community field trips, with county Medicaid funds to cover all expenses!

I didn't have to think long before signing up for that option. It was the perfect transitional answer to Mom's medical, social, spiritual, and psychological needs. The county even promised to provide free brand-new furniture, bed linens, towels, and a large wall clock.

In addition, there was a contingency plan in place. If Betty's overall condition worsened for any reason, there was a medical unit and nursing home on the grounds and she could easily transfer to that level of care temporarily, or permanently, depending on her specific care needs. Happy days were here again ... so we thought.

However, the best laid plans of mice and men sometimes go awry. Betty perked up slightly while a resident at this Christian center but chose not to engage in the life-energizing social activities. She also refused to attend worship services and preferred to sit in her room and watch TV all the time. She had this flat affect and seemed indifferent about life ... or about death. Betty reiterated the statement from prior years: "Sometimes, I just want to fall asleep and not wake up." Frequent visits from Rhonda, me, my family, and her sister Florence seemed to produce no positive effects. Just more of the same old depression.

I felt so helpless. I could do nothing to snap my mother out of this funk. It was so sad and so frustrating at the same time. It seemed the depression would continue indefinitely. Any attempts to improve Betty's quality of life were met with her depression-induced indifference. Nothing seemed to make her happy. There was no joy, no zest for living, no desire on her part to maintain personal hygiene or even to care about outward appearance. At mealtimes, Betty preferred to dine without conversation, and the other diners at Betty's roundtable weren't into socializing either.

Just once I hoped to see my mother smile, and smile because she *wanted to*, not just to maintain a social norm. Just once I hoped she would take delight in watching a funny program on TV, hear a joke and respond with laughter, sit outside and enjoy conversing with a fellow resident, brighten up at the sight of a gift received, or glow from a compliment directed toward her.

No, just that constant lifeless facial expression and desire to do nothing but sit and stare.

The Final Chapter

It started with a phone call from the facility staff that Betty was sent to the hospital for suspected aspiration pneumonia. And the rest of that hospital stay, about a week in duration, remains a blurry, unclear blotch in my memory bank. Betty was complaining of stomach distress, and the hospital staff chalked it up as a stomach virus with irritable bowels further aggravated by the stress and trauma of the hospitalization. Either way, Betty became weaker and weaker, ran a slight fever, had a slight heart murmur, and had "aspiration pneumonia" to boot. She was placed in the intensive care unit for closer observation. A few physicians were puzzled as to why Betty's condition had continued to decline and would not improve in any way. More stomach pain, more confusion, and more lethargy.

After a weekend in which Betty appeared stabilized and comfortable, Rhonda and I went back to our daily work routines. Betty was sleeping most of the time, and we were confident that in a few days she would be discharged from the hospital in favor of getting more rest back at the Christian care center.

One day, after work, I proceeded to the hospital for my usual nightly visit with Betty. I was greeted at the door by my sister and two physicians who shared that stark news that Betty was experiencing a perforated colon, that her system had gone septic, and that she was not expected to survive the rest of the evening!

They stated bluntly that surgery was no longer an option, and even if they operated to repair the perforation, Betty would not survive because the septic level had reached fatal proportions. There were no medical options left and, according to the physicians, Betty would not live long enough to see the next morning. It was around six in the evening when this news was shared. I felt weak-kneed and extremely helpless.

In a state of shock and disbelief, I remember filling with tears, turning slightly away, and uttering, "I didn't see this coming. There's nothing left to do?" The staff simply shook their heads, shrugged their shoulders, and offered coffee to soothe the pain of our newly initiated death vigil.

A Peaceful Good-Bye

Betty was only partially alert, and somehow I got the courage to say something positive. Fighting back the tears, I said, "Mom, you're going to fall asleep soon, but you'll wake up in heaven," my voice quivering in sadness and in disbelief at the sudden unexpected turn of events.

I remember speaking the Twenty-Third Psalm for Betty and praying aloud intermittently throughout the next few hours. There was a monitor near the bed that tallied periodic blood pressure readings, blood-oxygen levels, respiratory rates, etc. Betty eventually slipped into a deep sleep and then her breathing patterns became unnervingly familiar to me. They were the breathing patterns common to all the hospice patients I had witnessed over the years: patients who were in the actively dying phase. Only this time, it wasn't a hospice patient. It was my own mother who was actively dying. And now, it all seemed so surreal.

Once in a while, the bedside monitor alarm would chime, indicating that the heart rate was exceedingly low. The EKG lines were growing smaller and spaced farther apart. The inevitable end was near.

My sister and I rhythmically looked at Mom, then back at the vitals monitor as the telltale signs of approaching death were not to be denied. I prayed for Betty to join the saints in heaven. Rhonda and I cried a bit more. And then, in the peaceful privacy of that intensive care room, just before midnight, the monitors chirped for the last time.

It was all over. Now the silence … more silence … more silence … and one final prayer that God would gently receive Betty's soul into his glorious kingdom.

She was gone.

The Funeral

Betty indicated for years prior to her passing that she wanted to be cremated and did not want sadness to pervade the funeral home visitation. We tried our best to fulfill those wishes.

Just nine months after presenting my father's eulogy, Rhonda was once again at the same podium, in the same funeral home, giving a sincere and heartfelt address—this time in memory of her best friend and mother, Betty.

We all agreed that Betty did not have a mean bone in her body. She never told a lie, not even a "white lie." She never wished harm on anyone. She was meek and mild. Once the life of everyone's party, Betty withered away in those final years, succumbing to the terrible effects of chronic depression and a less than desirable quality of life. In her eighties, she lost the will to live and spent her final chapter of life counting the listless days before reaching the finish line.

God eventually granted Betty the desires of her fervent prayer: to fall asleep and not wake up again.

In prior years, nobody could have predicted that Betty, in the twilight of her life, would become reclusive, unemotional, lethargic, listless, and debilitated. The once effervescent "Betty Boop" had gradually, steadily, faded away—right along with the memories of her smile and sense of humor. How sad it was to observe the deterioration over the course of time.

So Helpless

Reflecting back upon the time of my mother's demise, I recall my persistent and relentless feelings of helplessness. I could do nothing to brighten my mother's sullen demeanor in those final days. As a result, I am constantly haunted by dreams of what could have been, had it not been for the devastating effects of that chronic depression.

My mother lost the will to live, and no "magic pill" could bring her back.

For many whose parents are declining toward death, helplessness becomes the overarching theme of all existence. It is this theme that will be examined in the next chapter.

Chapter 5

Addressing Spiritual Helplessness

The Serenity Prayer

God grant me the serenity
To accept the things I cannot change;
Courage to change the things I can;
And wisdom to know the difference.

Living one day at a time;
Enjoying one moment at a time;
Accepting hardships as the pathway to peace;
Taking, as He did, this sinful world
as it is, not as I would have it;
Trusting that He will make all things right
if I surrender to his will;
That I may be reasonably happy in this life
and supremely happy with Him forever in the next.
Amen[13]

Aside from the Lord's Prayer, the prayer listed above may be considered the most popular prayer among believers today. Reflecting back on my mother's journey toward death, feelings of helplessness continue to surface in my brain, but the serenity prayer brings comfort to my troubled soul.

Notice the phrase "to accept the things I cannot change," and later the line "Trusting that He will make all things right *if I surrender to His will"* (italics mine). These phrases encourage the one who is praying to acknowledge some basic truths.

- One can't control everything that happens.
- The most appropriate course of action is to yield to the will of the Omnipotent One.

If you are attentive to the seven spiritual themes I have outlined in this book, you may wonder why helplessness is not included in this list and why it does not appear as an eighth theme. This omission is deliberate on my part, because helplessness is a symptom related to the overarching spiritual theme of control, as outlined in chapter 3.

When we feel helpless, we perceive ourselves in a state of a control-less-ness. We feel there is nothing in our power to change or manipulate variables to bring more desirable outcomes. Our hands are tied, our choices are finite, and we feel boxed in by circumstances beyond our ability to influence or alter.

Your Predicament

If one or both of your parents is elderly and experiencing a diminished cognitive capacity, then helpless feelings will certainly prevail for you. Perhaps you have a parent who is experiencing the full-blown effects of Alzheimer's disease. Or perhaps one of your parents has not been officially diagnosed as having Alzheimer's yet is suffering from an advanced stage of dementia. Or perhaps, as in the case of my mother, one of your parents may be chronically depressed, bipolar, schizophrenic, or suffering from any wide array of behavioral disorders or mood disorders. What will you do? What *can* you do?

If you are like me, you view your parents' psychiatric deficiencies as something you'll try to fix. Or at least you might be able to tweak some of the environmental factors to produce an outcome more pleasing to your senses. However, at the end of the day, you can tweak and turn, change and create, manipulate and consult, and you are still left with a parent who will not be able to change, cognitively speaking, to be the person he or she was in yesteryear.

Recently, the spouse of one of my hospice patients pointed to his wife, now suffering with end-stage Alzheimer's, and lamented, "She died a few years back. That person lying there is not my wife. She's just a shell of the person she once was." He went on to grieve the loss of her "former" self: intelligent, energetic, romantic, and nurturing. "Now, all she does is sit there, or lie there ... she doesn't know who I am, and she can't even feed herself," he observed.

What *can* you do? The harsh reality is this: not much, really. As the Serenity Prayer further advises, all you can do is live "one day at a time" or, as the gentleman mentioned in the previous paragraph once retorted, "One hour at a time." His coping strategy was, and remains, to take each hour as it comes, not expecting more and not expecting less. He admits this is a passive coping strategy, but he has ceased making future plans as his sense of helplessness has become the norm.

Toward Patience and Acceptance

The greatest challenge you face if your loved one is cognitively impaired or behaviorally impaired in any way is to work toward patience and acceptance. You truly need to "accept the things you cannot change," or you will die trying to change them.

I went through great pain and anguish the day I realized that I could not transform my mother from her current rag doll existence back to her former bubbly self. How devastating it was to watch her forlorn or empty countenance, to make suggestions that were not even acknowledged by her, or to introduce a gift only to have it received by a blank stare. It was equally devastating to watch her vegetate, as my mother's preferred way to live was to sit in the recliner, smoke cigarettes, and focus only on reruns broadcast on television. I often wondered what was going on in that mind of hers—or what was not going on. Metaphorically speaking, the light was on, yet nobody was home.

It was enormously painful to witness this woman who once enjoyed being around dogs and kids yet now had no interest in her daughter's show dogs or her four grandchildren. She preferred isolation over and above interaction, stagnation over and above mobility, and frequent naps over and above any interest in the world around her.

If one or more of your parents is in this station in life, then I have great empathy for you. The recurring fantasy is to wave that magic wand and make it all better. Or you wish the pharmaceutical world could invent the magic pill to restore life and vitality to your parent's wilting frame. Or you pray for one last miracle, one last day, in which you can actually converse with your loved one who can respond back in an intelligent way.

During this time, personality changes can be dramatic. And those changes can be emotionally devastating for you. That once gentle caring mom may turn into a nasty, cursing, and miserable human being. Or that once proud family provider you call Dad is now incontinent of bowel and bladder and frequently tries to pull off his diaper when left alone for a minute or two. Or the parent who was the "sharp" one in the family now needs to be instructed on how to buckle a belt or tie a shoe. It is so painful to sit back and witness the deterioration, along with the disparaging feeling that there is no way to prevent the downward spiral from continuing.

Who Is in Charge?

Helplessness is not a comfortable feeling. Few people take comfort in this state of mind. However, it may be wise to think back upon those Bible stories you learned when you were a kid. If you are feeling helpless, you are actually in good company.

- Noah felt helpless when it started to rain (Genesis 7:7).

- Joseph felt helpless when he was in the pit and left for dead (Genesis 37:24).
- Moses felt helpless when the people rebelled in the wilderness (Exodus 16:1–3).
- Shadrack, Meshack, and Abednego felt helpless when they went into the fiery furnace (Daniel 3:19–23).
- David felt helpless when pursued by the mentally ill Saul (1 Samuel 20:1).
- The widow at Zarephath felt helpless when her son died (1 Kings 17:17).
- Elijah felt helpless when he went into the desert and prayed to die (1 Kings 19:4).
- Jonah felt helpless when he was swallowed by the great fish (Jonah 1:17).
- The Southern Kingdom felt helpless when conquered by the Babylonians (Daniel 1:1–3).
- The prophets, like Jeremiah, felt helpless when they proclaimed doomsday to the people (Jeremiah 13:15–16).
- The disciples of Jesus felt helpless when hiding behind closed doors on Easter Sunday night (John 20:19).
- Zechariah felt helpless when he lost his ability to speak (Luke 1:22).
- Paul felt helpless when he lost his vision (Acts 9:9).

There are many other biblical examples of men and women who once felt helpless, **yet God answered their helplessness by empowering them *all*** to trust in divine mercy and to rise above all their earthly challenges for the greater glory!

Remember, the psalmist proclaims, "The eyes of the Lord are on the righteous and his ears are open to their cry … Many are the afflictions of the righteous, but the Lord rescues them from them all." (Psalm 34:15, 19 NRSV) And don't forget the well-known words of St. Paul. "We know that in all things God works for the good of those who love him" (Romans 8:28).

Never Truly Helpless

The biblical witness affirms time and time again that you are *never truly helpless* when you have God at your side. Somehow, someway, the Lord guides you through the darkest of circumstances, even if the Lord needs to carry you, as indicated in the familiar "Footprints" poem.

It may seem counterintuitive, but the remedy for helplessness is surrender, which involves precisely acknowledging the things and issues you cannot change and turning all your worries and concerns over to the only One who can change the outcome.

In the end, when all is said and done, the ultimate outcome will be the passing of your parents from this world to the next. To which I sincerely and humbly respond, "Is that the worst thing that could happen?"

Someday, the Lord of all life will call your parent(s) from the threshold of death to the gates of eternal glory. (Read John 14:1–6.) Will that be a bad thing? Or will that be the form of healing you can live with, and die with, until your great reunion with them at the end of the age?

According to the book of Revelation, all things become new in the afterlife (Revelation 21). Therefore, why not begin entrusting your parent(s) to the One who will completely restore all existence in the future? And this restoration may take place in the near future, for all we know.

Your Current Pain

I realize that my words may do little to comfort you *now* in the midst of your feelings of helplessness, grief, and emotional pain. But remember faith is always forward-looking. Faith strains forward to what lies ahead (Philippians 3:13–14). Faith anticipates rainbows from storms, relief from suffering, renewed power to the powerless, and even new life from death.

During a quiet moment, read Matthew 5:3–10 (commonly known as the beatitudes). Then consider how "future oriented" these statements are from the lips of Christ. According to Jesus, those who mourn *will be comforted;* those who hunger and thirst for righteousness *will be filled;* the merciful *will be shown mercy;* and the pure in heart *will see God.* These are all future-oriented concepts and visions. If you believe, as I do, that God fulfills all promises, then the best is yet to come! Or to coin a popular phrase, "You ain't seen nothing yet." A greater glory is just around the corner for you—and for your parents.

Toward Serenity and Acceptance

If you are feeling helpless now in the face of your aging parents, please remember what I did when my parents were declining beyond my control: I simply accepted the reality.

Try every day to spiritually accept the things you cannot change, to change the things you can, and to find the wisdom to differentiate between the two. Yes, that Serenity Prayer can go a long way in helping you cope with those many variables that God alone should handle, not you.

Someday, your parents *will* get to the finish line of their earthly journey; and when they do, please resolve to have no regrets, no remorse, and no guilt. Do the best you can right now. And through it all, keep complete faith and trust in the Author of Life. There will come a day when your loved ones' names will be "called" to the eternal destination of souls. Embrace that reality, and celebrate the paradise into which they will be welcomed, by the grace of God.

Rev. Dr. Jack DiMatteo

Looking Ahead

Having considered the spiritual dimensions of saying farewell to your elderly parents (Part 1 of this book), it is now appropriate to explore ways in which you can fortify yourself with spiritual energy for the journey ahead. Part 2 of this book will provide tips and insights for your spiritual strengthening.

Part 2

Spiritual Strengthening As You Approach the Finish Line

Chapter 6

Spiritual Tips for Your Survival

As stated earlier in this book, you may be in for a long journey as you guide your parents to their earthly finish line. Perhaps your parents have quite some time left before they meet their Maker. They may be in fairly good physical shape while aging slowly and steadily, or they may be facing long-term illnesses that will require your assistance for the duration of several years. Whatever the circumstances, it is helpful for you to be prepared for the long run as you pray for wisdom and endurance along the way.

Reflecting on my own experience, as well as the experiences of countless "hospice" families I have observed over the years, I have created some spiritual tips for your future survival. Read them carefully, and may you gain additional wisdom and insight for the days ahead. I refer to these tips as "The Ten Commandments for Spiritual Survival."

The Ten Commandments for Spiritual Survival

1. Acknowledge the Sovereignty of God

If you are a God-fearing person, then you need to acknowledge the sovereignty of God and respect the Lord's will in all circumstances. If there is one message that comes through loudly and clearly in this book, it is an invitation to respect God's timetable in all of life's endeavors. You can plan forever, and you can make wonderful arrangements for the future, but the ultimate outcome rests in the hands of God.

Please recall the insights I provided in chapter 1. Among those is that there is only a finite number of variables over which you can have direct control in the lives of your aging parents. Your plan A sometimes quickly dissolves into your plan B. Then, in the blink of an eye, plan B segues right into plan C, and before you know it, you are already on plans X, Y, and Z because circumstances can change in a heartbeat. This volatility becomes a stark reality, for example, if one of your parents suddenly falls at home and must deal with a fall-related injury. An injury of this magnitude could throw a sizeable monkey wrench right into a cog of a previously well-organized life. Suddenly, your well-ordered plans fly right out of the well-ordered window.

Please understand I am not encouraging a plan-less, fly-by-the-seat-of-your-pants kind of adventure. After all, it *is* necessary to engage in goal-oriented, end-of-life care planning for/with your elderly parents (as in the old adage "People don't plan to fail; they just fail to plan"). However, your best-laid plans must include a realistic contingency for flexibility and adaptability in the event that circumstances unfold in a truly unforeseen fashion. (I have yet to witness an elderly person's systematic and totally predictable waltz through life. There will be frequent twists and turns along the way that will require course corrections and adaptability for everyone involved in the process.)

With this in mind, please resolve to acknowledge the Lord's omnipotence and sovereignty in all aspects of life. As stated in chapter 5, the Serenity Prayer places all of this in proper perspective—there are things you *can* change, there are things you *cannot* change, and you desperately need the wisdom to differentiate between the two. Perhaps the greatest prayer you will ever utter is "thy will be done," thus acknowledging God's authority and majesty in all things—earthly and supernaturally. In the wisdom of the Scriptures, it is written, "My times are in your hand, O Lord" (Psalm 31:15).

Once you acknowledge that God is in charge and that God has your best interests in mind, you can rest assured that you *will* reach the earthly finish line with your parents, and the journey along the way will be much healthier and happier when you yield to God's plans. Otherwise, life for you will consist of an endless series of kicking and screaming and running uphill for most of the trek.

Which would you prefer: a life lived "in the flow" of God's grace or a life lived in desperation and stubbornness while trying to achieve your own goals and objectives? I am sure you already know the answer to that question.

2. Daily Read from a Study Bible or Application Bible

"Your word is a lamp to my feet and a light for my path" (Psalm 119:105). These words poignantly express the necessity of seeking wisdom and guidance from above. The Lord wants to instruct you, guide, you, and lead you into the future. Seeking God's wisdom is a great way to begin to navigate through the complex world of caring for the needs of your aging parents. I strongly suggest that you obtain a Bible that contains study aids and application materials in order to invigorate your Bible reading.

You are at a time in your life when you greatly need divine wisdom to address the myriad of decisions required for your parents' care. Why not consult the ultimate Source of all wisdom? I suggest that you begin your quest by utilizing the recommended Bible readings I provide in chapter 7. Immerse yourself in the Word. Pray before, during, and after your Bible study time.

I advise you to find a Bible concordance in order to research specific topics of concern as they present themselves in your life. Internet search engines are phenomenal in this regard as well. My personal preference has always been to read as many study aids as possible in order to gain more in-depth insights and knowledge regarding ways in which the Lord is speaking to me and my particular circumstances. In the process, I try to be as open-minded as possible in order to objectively examine these circumstances as they play out in daily living.

This may sound trite, but whenever I am faced with challenging endeavors, I often wonder, *What would Jesus do?* Then, other related questions follow in sequential thought. *How would Jesus react to that pompous doctor? How would Jesus respond to situations evoking anger, frustration, sadness, or grief? How would Jesus juggle the demands of daily living?* You will not have to be overly creative to discover the answers to these direct questions.

The Scriptures place life in proper perspective, and God's Word serves as a great blueprint for daily living. Think of it this way: if you had the opportunity to seek the wisdom of the wisest being on a daily basis, wouldn't you afford yourself the luxury of this opportunity? Well, in God's Word, you will discover and rediscover timeless wisdom for all areas of daily living.

Some people are intimidated by the Bible and do not know where to begin reading. Others simply find the Bible too complex for comprehension. Still others complain that the biblical message is outdated or irrelevant for today's world. Quite the contrary! This is why I advise the use of study Bibles, which can be read for personal application and edification. When one reads Bible verses along with their accompanying reference tools, it is like sitting down with a Bible scholar who can explain each passage related to its historicity, context, and theological significance. Suddenly, everything becomes more meaningful and useful for daily reflection.

Recently, one of my hospice patients shared that he had a growing thirst for Bible reading but did not know how to get started or where to begin. I gently guided George (not his actual name) in the process. I recommended that he obtain a study Bible. To convince him, one day I had George page through my study Bible while I pointed out all the reference tools, maps, cross-references, application essays, biographies, and other materials I regularly use to assist with comprehension and application. (In retrospect, I must have looked like a Bible salesman, but I wanted George to know how Bible study had greatly influenced me and changed my life around for the better.)

I suggested that George begin reading the gospel of Mark, for starters, as Mark is generally considered the first of the gospels to be written. I also explained the simplicity of Mark's account, as juxtaposed against the theological complexity of the gospel of John. Before leaving that day, I stressed the importance of Bible reading for personal application and encouraged George to pray before, during, and after Bible study.

Not long after my Bible "show and tell" session, I visited George again and noticed that he had indeed obtained a study Bible of his own. (Note: in today's world, one can even borrow a study Bible from the local public library!) He was glowing with excitement. "I understand this translation!" He added, "It is like reading the Bible in everyday language, without the thees and thous that used to throw me off course. I actually understand what I'm reading."

I could see the excitement and enthusiasm in George's eyes. He was a kid in the candy store!

I promised I would arrange for George to receive daily devotional materials to arrive at his residence via the mail service, so that George could read selected Bible verses with accompanying commentaries each day.

On a subsequent visit, George proudly ushered me into his study room. I was deeply impressed by the setup: a study Bible, a book holder embracing his study Bible, a daily devotional booklet next to that, and a notepad upon which George jotted questions, insights, and prayer concerns! He had created an attractive "study corner" and shared with me how the Bible had come alive for him. He explained how he felt closer to God now, and after seventy-five years of living in darkness, he now felt that God's Word had shed a new light into his life. I walked away from that visit glowing with happiness for George's newly found love affair with the Word of God.

It can happen for you too! Please nurture yourself with the Holy Scriptures. It is never too late to start reading the Bible. Those daily Bible readings will change your life (as they did for George) and you will find inspirational strength for your journey ahead. Bible reading can, and should, become a key ingredient in your daily "survival" plan!

3.   Daily Make Time for Prayer and Meditation

This commandment follows closely on the heels of the previous directive: Bible study and prayer always go hand-in-hand. It's like the old song lyrics: "Love and marriage: You can't have one without the other."[14] God's Word often speaks in the quiet, reflective moments of prayer.

So often, people think of prayer as unidirectional. They think that prayer is all about our telling God what we want, how we want it, when we want it, etc. Perhaps this is part of the process, but I lean heavily on the "listening" side of prayer. I try to be quiet and listen for the "still, small voice" (1 Kings 19:12) of the Lord encouraging me and directing my steps. I often engage in centering prayer, which involves simply sitting and "being" with God, without having a verbal or written agenda. I sit and "think" with God by my side, and I ask the Lord to bring new insights and new pieces of wisdom into my soul. It works! I am pleased to share that this has joyfully occurred on so many occasions, especially whenever I felt stuck in a problem or personal challenge.

Go ahead and pray, fervently. Prayer invites the one praying to dig deeper into the soul and to truly listen for the voice of God. Someone once gave me tremendous advice that I try to follow in everyday life: when faced with major choices or a complicated set of circumstances, *never* make quick decisions. Take time to pray about it, think about it, and share it with the Lord. Over the course of time, new insights and strategies will surface. That process has never, ever let me down. And I suggest the same for you.

4.   Get Involved with a Faith Community

Participation in a faith community is a two-way street. You nurture others, and you receive nurturing as well. However, be on the lookout. If your parents' needs are becoming greater, and you find yourself attending more to their needs, then you may feel extremely limited in your ability to nurture others in your faith community at this time. You may feel that you need to be more on the receiving end of the nurturing spectrum. And that is all right ... for now. You can't devote hours and hours of volunteer work in your faith community when your own parents need more from you. After all, there are seasons in life when family demands become paramount, and this may be one of those seasons for you. Once, St. Paul advised, "If anyone does not provide for his relatives, and especially for his immediate family, he has denied the faith and is worse than an unbeliever" (1 Timothy 5:8).

What I am stressing here is that being involved in a faith community definitely implies your volunteer service of some kind, but this may be a time in your life when volunteers need to knock on *your* door to lend a helping hand. You need to be the receiver, not the giver, for a while as you seek to address various caregiving demands.

Your faith community is truly the "body of Christ" in the world. And as Paul so aptly states, if one part of the body suffers, then we all suffer (1 Corinthians 12:26ff). As members of the body of Christ, all Christians are encouraged to help others in their times of need. It may be your time of need, and the faithful body of Christ needs to rally for your support!

I admire congregations that have care ministries in place, such as a "new mother" ministry, a grief ministry, and a hospital visiting ministry. It is my hope and prayer that one of those caring ministries will reach out to you during this stressful time. Please share your burdens with your pastor or other religious leaders so that the body of Christ can identify your *specific* needs, lift you up in prayer, and respond in specific loving ways that will provide greatly needed relief and support.

The key is obviously revealing your needs to those who can assist you! The world is full of "rugged individual" types who do not feel comfortable asking for assistance. You do not have to be one of the rugged individualists. You do not have to be a martyr in trying to carry your cross alone!

If there is one thing that bothers me, it is observing someone who complains that neighbors are unresponsive, that the faith community is ignoring the situation, or that family members have turned away; however, the reality is the "stressed-out" individual never asked for assistance in the first place!

Once, a woman complained to me that her church family was ignoring her needs at this time in her life. But upon further examination, I discovered that she never revealed those needs to anyone who could offer assistance. I guess she assumed that her pastor and church friends were able to supernaturally read her mind and respond to any of her concerns in a moment's notice. She probably assumed there was a pervasive clairvoyance within the body of believers when, in reality, the church family did not even have a clue as to what this woman was experiencing. With this woman's permission, I shared her concerns with her family pastor, and within a short time, this woman had more help than she knew what to do with!

The church is the body of Christ. Please do not hesitate to tell your pastor or others in the church family that you are in great need of prayer and assistance. I have pleasantly discovered that most church families are enthusiastically willing to respond to the needs of those around them, and they can respond to your needs.

You may recall what Jesus said one day. "When I was hungry you gave me food" (Matthew 25). The listeners were befuddled and responded, "When did we see You hungry?" Jesus responded, "What you did for the least of these you did for me" (Matthew 25:40). You may not realize this right now, but having the added responsibilities of caring for aging parents qualifies *you* to be included in the list of the "least of these." You may be tired, depressed, and overwhelmed—all the more reason to receive assistance and encouragement from your faith family.

5. Discover Your Parents' Wishes … and Address Them

It is never too early to ask your parents what they really want. What are their wishes for end-of-life care? How do they wish to spend their remaining days? Do they feel comfortable having health-care professionals visit their home? Do they feel comfortable with a live-in aide? What are their wishes regarding resuscitation or heroic measures intended to save their lives? Have they considered an advanced directive or living will? How do they feel about prearranging funerals? Do they wish to have viewing times at a funeral home? Do they have family burial plots? Is cremation being considered?

I realize that there are multitudes of questions to be addressed, and in some family systems, these issues are pushed aside as too sensitive to discuss openly. As British sociologist Roman Krznaric recently observed, "Death is more distant from the Western mind today than at any other point in history … [the subject of death] has become the ultimate taboo topic of conversation, the perfect way to create an awkward silence."[15] He adds, "We … are surrounded by a culture of silence that needs to be broken. There is little to be lost, and much to be gained, from embracing [the subject of] death and letting it be heard upon our lips."[16] Indeed, death-related issues need to be faced by everyone in the family system, and the sooner they are addressed, the better!

As you have read in chapter 2, my father had his moments of stubbornness and downright noncompliance in response to several suggestions made by various health-care professionals. However, he paid meticulous attention to his preplanned funeral arrangements. Long before his death, he knew what he wanted and took the initiative to plan out his entire funeral. He scheduled an appointment with the funeral director and selected his own casket, chose the prayer cards he wanted, decided upon the visitation hours for the viewing. He even composed his own obituary and made suggestions for the postburial family luncheon. How is *that* for specificity?

I was greatly relieved when my father preplanned his funeral. In this way, I knew exactly what he wanted. And when the time eventually arrived, we all carried out his wishes to the letter.

This is a time when you may need to have a few serious discussions with your parents. Be careful though. They may feel as if you are trying to hurry them to the finish line. It is important to stress that you sincerely want to honor their wishes and their desires. These sensitive subject areas need to be addressed carefully and sincerely in order to avoid potential misunderstandings in the future.

Recently, I witnessed a family in which the siblings were arguing constantly after their mother passed away. Everybody had differing views as to what their mother wanted. One brother said that his mother wanted a closed casket. The sister disagreed, stating that her mother wanted a traditional viewing. Then, there were fights over the kind of religious service to be conducted, as family members were of varying denominational affiliations. The whole thing was a mess, and several of the tensions were caused by earlier avoidance. When the mother was still alive, she refused to discuss these "personal" matters and the adult children were just as content to sweep the issues under the rug.

All was fine and quiet until the day the mother died unexpectedly, leaving her children behind to sort out the choices and to fight over conflicting ideologies. There was not a happy ending or peaceful resolution to this dilemma. I witnessed the siblings giving one another the silent treatment during the funeral as they dispersed to neutral corners. How sad.

If you or your parents are uncomfortable discussing these things, then please consider enlisting the help of a professional, such as a social worker, counselor, or chaplain, to assist in sorting out the issues and arriving at some definitive set of agreed-upon expectations.

There is a document that I highly recommend for families who want to explore their parents' wishes regarding end-of-life care. It is called "The Five Wishes" and covers more specific ground than does a typical advanced directive.[17] One can even specify the genre of music to be played softly at one's deathbed experience! Check out this document on the Internet. I advise once more, however, the enlistment of health-care professionals if these end-of-life issues are too uncomfortable for you and/or your parents to discuss alone.

The bottom line: it is well worth the effort to determine, as specifically as possible, your parents' wishes for end-of-life care, funeral arrangements, etc. In this way, you can honor their wishes and rest assured that their needs are being addressed delicately, sensitively, and personally—right up to and including the time of the funeral. Broaching these subject areas now may prevent loads of painful emotional stress later on.

6. Learn As Much As You Can about Your Parents

Years ago, there was a terrific book series published for new parents who were searching for guidance related to parenting. Each book's title began with the words "What to Expect …" One volume centered on what to expect when the child is an infant. Another book concentrated on what to expect during the toddler years, and so on.

Psychologists agree that whenever one begins an unfamiliar journey, it is comforting and less stress producing if one is instructed on typical patterns (e.g., "what to expect"). Realistic expectations help to avoid unwanted surprises later on.

The same holds true for you. If one of your parents is experiencing a certain medical condition, it is extremely helpful to understand what to expect in regard to typical signs and symptoms of the illness. As the old expression says, "Forewarned is fore-armed." Learn how you can provide the ultimate comfort and support in specific illness-related situations.

You can be a much better caregiver or care provider when you are informed about the illness and its effects. For example, I am working with a family engaged in caring for the family matriarch at home. She has an end-stage Alzheimer's condition and the entire family has benefitted from learning what to expect, and what not to expect, as the advanced Alzheimer's stage wears on. They are realistic about the mother's cognitive challenges. They know that correcting their mother over and over again serves no useful purpose. Above all, they have learned how to be a bit more patient and flexible whenever the family matriarch behaves in an unconventional way.

How did they learn about Alzheimer's disease? They did their homework. They searched topics on the Internet and gathered books from the library. They discussed issues with health-care professionals, and some members of the family are now attending a support group for caregivers. Each person in the family system now affirms this reality: advanced insight as to "what to expect" has greatly assisted the family unit in sensitively addressing the matriarch's specific needs. They also learned how to make the home safer in order to reduce the probability that the matriarch will fall or become injured in any way.

Please take the time to learn about the specific health concerns facing your parents, and then resolve to have realistic expectations. I often explain to families, "If someone in your family has one leg, would you expect that person to run one hundred meters in ten seconds? If someone else in the family has a visual deficit, would you place obstacles and toys right in the middle of the home's busy pathways? Of course not." Yet so many families do not take the time to adequately assess the needs of their aging parents and then have unrealistic expectations later. They expect too much, and they get frustrated and agitated when those unrealistic expectations are not satisfied. Worse yet, they are surprised when accidents happen involving the aging parents, because nobody in the family took the time to establish a safer environment in which the accidents could have been prevented.

I recall the time my father arrived home after a recovery stay in the local rehab facility. A visiting nurse came out to assess the environment and to make suggestions for safety, etc. She made a simple suggestion, but it was in an area that I had previously overlooked. She suggested a handrail bar to be installed next to the toilet—a terrific idea, and one I had totally missed until her suggestion was vocalized.

Perhaps you need to make a more careful assessment of your parents' needs. Is the home cluttered, with pathways inviting future slips or falls? Is the stove safe for your parents' daily use? Would an emergency alert wristband or pendant be appropriate in the event of a future fall or other emergency? Are there neighbors or others who can be available in the event of a crisis when you are at work or out of town? Is one of your parents telling you he or she is fine but in your heart of hearts you know that is not the case? Are there issues of forgetfulness that might become seriously dangerous later, such as the parent who walks away with the stove still burning or the outside grill still flaming?

Here's one to consider: have you ever observed one of your parents trying to put on a pair of pants? That can be a dangerous endeavor too! Once, my mother had a serious accident when she was alone. Instead of sitting on the bed while putting on her pants, she stood up. When placing one leg into the pants, she lost her balance, fell, and broke her femur. (That resulted in emergency surgery and weeks of physical therapy.) Perhaps the accident could have been avoided had she learned a safer way to put on pants while sitting down instead of standing!

Learn about safety. Learn about medications and illness-specific symptoms. Learn what to expect as your parents journey through the aging process. Learn how you can help to make your parents more comfortable as they journey through life.

7. Get Legal Paperwork Organized As Soon As Possible

This is another one of those potentially sensitive issues for some family systems. Some parents might feel as if their adult children are rushing them to the cemetery whenever someone in the family encourages the completion of legal paperwork related to end-of-life issues. However, as in other areas of life, advanced planning in the present helps to avoid seriously painful circumstances later.

It is time for you and/or other members of the family to begin gathering critical documents that will come in handy later on. For example, someone in the family should be designated as the power of attorney regarding financial matters (in the event that one or both of the parents become physically or mentally incapacitated) so that financial obligations can be addressed and financial plans maintained.

I recently witnessed an event whereby a parent had a severe stroke and could not function physically or cognitively. The adult child was then saddled with the responsibility of maintaining the parent's financial obligations, even though the parent was unable to sign checks or other legal documents. The whole thing blew up when others in the family accused the adult child of mismanaging funds and "taking over" without having obtained the prior consent of the parent. (There were other serious issues that I will not reveal at this time.) However, if the adult child had been predesignated as the power of attorney, there would have been considerably less anxiety/ anger expressed by other members of the extended family.

Although financial management is a critical piece to address, it is just as critical to plan ahead regarding future health-care decisions. It is imperative that the parents designate a health-care proxy who can execute the parents' wishes in the event that they later become cognitively incapacitated and unable to verbalize health-care preferences.

Preparing these legal documents need not be expensive, since the forms can be downloaded for free or for a nominal cost via the

Internet. When completing a generic template, be careful to specify the state in which the parent resides, as elder laws vary from state to state.

When my parents were declining rapidly, I obtained various legal template forms from the Internet and then assisted my parents in completing them. I also suggested that my sister serve as codurable power of attorney along with me as we interviewed our parents to determine what they wanted for the future. Eventually, we had the legal documents notarized, with several copies available for doctors, bank officials, and other relevant parties.

Your particular situation may not be as cut and dry as ours, especially if there are conflicts within the family and/or disagreements regarding future wishes. If that is the case, I strongly advise legal consultation for completion of the official documentation. It is advisable to have an attorney review the paperwork before it is signed and/or notarized, for obvious legal protections.

It probably goes without saying, but similar legal advice needs to be sought whenever the parents initiate a last will and testament, with special attention to the designation of someone to serve as an executor and another to act as alternate executor.

The bottom line is that it does no good to delay the process of initiating and completing the legal paperwork relative to these sensitive yet critical matters for the parents.

8.   Enlist the Assistance of Professionals

This commandment follows closely on the heels of the seventh commandment previously described. Professional assistance and guidance can be found along several levels and for various issues facing your aging parents. You do not have to navigate these waters alone. That is why there are health-care professionals, clergy, attorneys, therapists, and others available to offer guidance in these matters. As to legal issues, there is an entire branch of legal specialists who concentrate on "elder law" circumstances. They can offer much-needed advice relative to the complicated matters involving tax strategies, long-term health insurance, will, estate planning, etc. They will also advise on delicate matters involving your parents' possible gifting options while they are still alive and provide warnings respectful of the Medicaid "look-back" period relative to asset allocation.

It is probably a good idea to have a joint family meeting involving your parents, you, your siblings, and a qualified professional to facilitate and mediate the proceedings. In this way, sensitive issues can be discussed openly and honestly while different family members are afforded a voice and participation in the overall planning process. The professional mediator has the opportunity to address/resolve potential conflict issues as they arise in the family system. If conducted appropriately, the family meeting (or meetings) will keep everyone on the same page with respect to planning and expectations—and nobody will feel left out of the process. I have discovered professional mediators to be especially adept at empowering the quieter members of the family to speak their minds, thus shielding the more timid family members from being verbally bullied or coerced by the more powerful personalities in the family system. The end result is everybody is heard and respected in the moderated open forum and the meetings result in definitive action plans with concrete communication strategies.

9.   Work Collaboratively with Siblings

It is advisable to agree upon one member of the family who can serve as the "captain," or lead person, to represent the family in communication with key health-care providers. For instance, if a parent is receiving care at home from a team of professionals (such as hospice home care), the professionals do not have the time to telephone eight different family members with the same periodic updates and/or recommendations. It is much more practical for the health-care team members to relay information to one designated family representative who can then disseminate information to the rest of the family system via e-mail updates, text messages, and the like. Of course, communication is the key. Whoever is designated as the family captain must agree to accept responsibility for providing timely updates to the rest of the family as situations change—and circumstances may change rapidly, especially if one or both of the parents are hospitalized!

A few years ago, my elderly uncle was experiencing several medical problems that involved frequent trips to doctors, hospitals, and other professionals. He resided over one hundred miles away from the rest of the family and had no children of his own. By the grace of God, a neighbor befriended my uncle and then volunteered to serve as the key communicator to our family whenever circumstances changed. We received daily e-mail updates and found it practical to share ideas via the e-mail loop regarding future care strategies. This system worked—and can work for your family too.

We're blessed to be living in a "communication" era; there is simply no excuse not to keep in touch with other family members. Technology now allows for live video conferencing via home computers, tablets, and cell phones so that family members, separated geographically, can have timely and essential family meetings. Thankfully, the days of jet-setting and running through airports are long gone. Please avail yourself of the luxury of instant communication with other family members so that crucial decisions never become inappropriately delayed.

Families usually function better when duties and responsibilities are divided up with an agreed-upon plan for the future. This idea does not contradict my earlier suggestion of appointing a family captain. Instead, it assures the family captain will not take the *sole* burden and run the risk of burnout. For example, one member of the family can serve as the "communication captain"; another may live geographically closer to the parent(s) for transportation to doctor appointments, shopping, banking, etc.

I stress once more that health-care professionals can assist in facilitating an agreed-upon division of labor throughout the family system. Democracies work best in governments and in families, so try to achieve a good system of checks and balances, division of labor, communications liaisons, etc.—all under the supervision of a qualified social worker or mediator to ensure that the "system" is working as structured and agreed upon by members of the family.

You might be reading this and envisioning a chaotic nightmare if duties and responsibilities become delegated among *your* siblings. Perhaps some members of your family do not get along well with the others. Or perhaps certain siblings in the family are perceived as distant or unreliable and cannot be counted upon to rise to the occasion during times of crisis. In fact, you may be reading this and remembering other occasions in history when you—and only you—stepped up to the plate to address the timely issues facing your elderly parents, and the thought of involving other family members in the process now sends shivers up and down your spine. Well, there may be truth in all that; however, that is all the more reason to enlist the aid of qualified professionals who can make concrete recommendations and facilitate healthier family cooperation for the days ahead. It does no good to be a lone ranger in the heat of the moment. You only set yourself up for blame and/or criticism in the future if you shut out other family members during this sensitive time of change and stress.

I once heard a story about ten men in a rowboat. The boat sprang a leak, and eight of the men were frantically bailing out the water. Buckets were flying, water was flying, and the eight men were in a panic. Meanwhile, two men were sitting calmly in the back of the boat, just sitting there doing nothing. They hadn't a worry in the world and seemed generally disinterested in the crisis at hand. Then, one of the sitters turned to the other and said, "Aren't you glad that hole is not on *our end* of the boat?"

When it comes to caring for elderly parents and facing their potential demise, please realize that you and your siblings are all in the same boat together! It is essential that you learn to work together at a time like this, even if you have to hire a professional who can teach you how to work cooperatively and faithfully toward common goals and objectives. Assuming there is no hole in the boat, you all want to be rowing in the same direction without a mutiny on your hands!

10. Give Thanks to God—Always!

Once in a while, I turn on the evening news and view scenes of what has become the aftermath of a disaster: a tornado touched down in Oklahoma and wiped out an entire trailer park, rampant forest fires in California destroyed hundreds of homes, or hurricane floodwaters washed away coastline dwellings. In fact, not long ago, my own state of New Jersey experienced widespread damage as the result of Superstorm Sandy causing millions to be without power and thousands of others completely homeless. What I find remarkable is the faith and resilience expressed by the survivors of these natural disasters. There always seems to be someone interviewed by a television reporter at the disaster site—someone who just lost a home and all earthly possessions. Yet this certain someone looks right into the interviewer's eyes and says, "We still have each other. We may have lost our things, but we still have our family, and our community, and our God!"

Survivors of natural disasters seem to find *something to be thankful for—even when the whole world is crumbling around them!* What an example for the rest of us. I am convinced that in all circumstances, no matter how bleak, there is *something* to be thankful for. And that blessing, whatever it is, can be the one sustaining factor toward healthy survival and the renewal of hope for you and those around you.

If one of your parents is beginning to struggle physically and/or emotionally, you may feel like your whole world is falling apart.

You may be losing hope and faith. Injustice has knocked on your door, burst in, and decided to take up residence in your house for a longer period of time than you bargained for. Nonetheless, please do not give up on the future!

The key to survival is summed up in this tenth "survival" commandment: *Give thanks to God—always!* A thankful heart will fortify you and sustain you during a multitude of challenges that may come your way. There is always *something* for which to be thankful.

I think back to a time when my parents became needy, my job became demanding, and my kids became mischievous—all at the same time. However, I found a remedy for the stress. I would get in my Prayer Chair and begin to thank God for all of the blessings I had—and the list was endless. I would sit there and give thanks for my health, for my intellect, for caring people in my life, for quiet times, and above all, for God's grace and sustaining Spirit. While in the Prayer Chair, I kept reminding myself that life isn't always fair (at least not from my perspective) and that things do not always work out immediately. But in the end, everything does work out according to God's will and by his providential care. Back then, each time I gave thanks to God, I felt better!

One day, during an extremely stressful time, I read the words of St. Paul. "Let the peace of Christ rule in your heart ... and be thankful" (Philippians 3:15). Then I considered St. Paul's circumstances. He wrote those words while a prisoner in Rome. He was facing the death penalty for proclaiming Christ as Lord. Yet in those dark days, Paul truly had a thankful heart, giving thanks to God for using him as an instrument for evangelizing the world! Paul sat there, in chains, giving thanks to Almighty God—always! In the same letter to his dear friends at Philippi, Paul wrote, "Rejoice in the Lord always. I will say it again: Rejoice!" (Philippians 4:4). From where did all this gratitude come? Why the thankful heart? Why not bitterness for ending up in prison unjustly? The answer is simple. St. Paul, through the power of the Holy Spirit, made a conscious *choice* to be thankful because he knew that in every situation and in all circumstances, a thankful heart nurtures and sustains the soul to face any challenge, any obstacle, any hardship (even death itself) by the grace of God!

If you truly desire to survive the long journey of ushering your parents to their earthly end point, then resolve now to have a thankful heart and you will never be disappointed. Start by giving thanks to God for your parents.

Perhaps your parents are difficult to get along with right now. But remember they were the ones who worked hard and made sacrifices for you and the family years ago. They were the ones who tried their best when parenting you. (Although they made their share of parenting mistakes, they are only human, like the rest of us.) They were the ones who taught you valuable lessons and have impacted your personality to this day.

Give thanks to God that you are now in the position to respond to your parents with gratitude—by addressing their care needs in the here and now. In the poignant words of Roman Krznaric, "Our parents brought us into the world, and we can help them leave it with contentment and dignity, even if we have not always seen eye to eye."[18]

Give thanks to God that you are smart enough and caring enough to nurture your parents in their time of need. Give thanks to God that you can look beyond the petty disagreements or conflicts you may have had with your parents in the past, and you can now rise up to make a positive difference in their world and during their twilight years.

Remember there is always *something* to be thankful for, and a spirit of thanksgiving will get you and your parents to that grand and glorious day when the Lord says, "Come home, you good and faithful servants. The kingdom of heaven is waiting for you!"

Chapter 7

Biblical Insights on the Seven Spiritual Themes

God's Word has a lot to say regarding the seven spiritual themes I have outlined in chapter 3. As I accompanied my parents through the final days of their lives, I gained wisdom and spiritual strength from the study of Scripture, most notably the verses I share in this chapter. Back in those days, I continually searched for God's voice throughout the journey, and I found great comfort in Bible verses, which nurtured and sustained me. Most importantly, I *continue* to devote considerable time each day for Bible reading, reflection, and meditation as I seek to *apply* the age-old principles of biblical insight to everyday living.

My advice to anyone who is preparing to say farewell to parents is to devote adequate time each day toward seeking wisdom from above. "Do not rely on your own understanding" (Proverbs 3:5) and "Do not be wise in your own eyes" (Proverbs 3:7). It is quite humbling to acknowledge your own limited wisdom while deferring to the will of the Divine Creator, who most certainly has deeper insights into the matters at hand.

This chapter contains suggested Bible readings and several application questions pertinent to the readings. The application questions are often rhetorical or open-ended as to invite personal reflections based on your specific concerns. Don't worry about finding the "correct" answers to the questions, since God will reveal insights to you over the course of time. Wisdom is gained through insight, reflection, prayer, and the seeking of God's all-knowing Spirit.

Common sense beckons you to devote some quiet, nondistracted time each day for reading, reflecting, and praying. Do not rush your time with God. Find your "space" where you can be alone with God and select a time that works for you. For some, early-morning reflections work best; for others, end-of-the-day devotions are more conducive to the spiritual integration of the entire day's journey.

It may be helpful to journalize your thoughts and insights. You may even consider writing out the words of your prayers for subsequent reflection and renewal.

Read and listen attentively to God's way of addressing you. Above all, be open-minded to new insights and sparkling new revelations gained through prayer and meditation. Feel free to structure your journey with spiritual goals and objectives, yet be open to the creative twists and turns that God has in store for you.

Methodology

You may wish to explore the seven spiritual themes in correlation with the seven days of the week. One strategy would be to address only one Scripture passage from each of the themes daily and proceed to cycle through the suggested readings. For instance, on day 1, you might read the first Bible verse from the authority theme. On day 2, read the first Bible verse from the control theme, etc. In this manner, you will cycle through five to six weeks of devotions from a broader perspective. Or you may choose to explore one complete theme for an entire week, while focusing daily on the application questions for that theme only. This allows for seven weeks of concentrated study and reflection. For some, it might be helpful to jump right into a specific spiritual theme, such as the isolation theme, if that appears to be most relevant to your particular situation at the time. There is great flexibility in how you might tackle the issues contained in this chapter.

Finally, in addition to your Bible readings, reflections, prayers, journals, and meditations based on the application questions, feel free to discuss the issues with a friend, a spouse, a counselor, or a pastor. I remember, back in the days of addressing my parents' needs, I gained great insight and consolation whenever I could share my thoughts and concerns with others who offered their patience, love, wisdom, and unconditional acceptance of my circumstances.

As you have probably discovered, not everyone is interested in your problems, and not everyone has the patience to be helpful. However, over time, you will discover those who are particularly nurturing in your life. Seek them out; they want to be helpful and encouraging. Find those who will listen with nonjudgmental empathy. Best of all, find those who can pray right along with you to invoke God's sustaining grace.

One final note: lean into these Bible verses. Jump in with all your heart and mind. Do not shy away from the issues and do not try to protect your emotions. If you need to cry, go ahead and cry. If you need to laugh, go ahead and laugh. If you feel anger welling up inside you, acknowledge the anger and try to discover ways, with God's grace, to work through whatever unpleasant feelings come to the surface. It is extremely therapeutic to acknowledge and accept feelings and emotions as they come along. This is part of the healing process. Let it happen! You will not find healing if you avoid the emotions, deny the emotions, or find creative ways to mask the emotions. Pray for the courage to face the emotions head on, and then take God's guiding hand, which will lead you through to a spiritually healthier existence.

1. Authority

1. Read Exodus 20:12 (Honor Your Father and Mother)
   - Other than on Father's Day or Mother's Day, when can you express love and honor for your parents? How can you demonstrate that love?

- Can you respect your parents' wishes, even if you disagree with them? How can you demonstrate this respect to them?
- When was the last time you said, "I love you" to either of your parents? Was it difficult? It is difficult to say those words? Why?
- When was the last time you prayed with your parents? Was that difficult? Can you initiate prayer with them now? Why? Why not?
- When have you thanked God for your parents? Do your parents know that you lift them up in prayer?
- Have you asked others to pray for or with your parents?

2. Read Genesis 21:1–38 (The Jacob/Esau Story)
   - Have there been times when you, like Jacob, have manipulated your parents into certain decisions/actions?
   - Do you often twist the truth or tell white lies in your parents' presence so as to not worry them?
   - Were there any recent "power plays" you initiated, like strong-arming your parents into a living arrangement that was better for you but not necessarily better for them?
   - When was the last time you tried to "pull the wool" over your parents' eyes? Did they perceive your plan? If so, what was their reaction? Your reaction?
   - Are your parents making their own decisions, or are *you* calling all the shots?
   - Do you ever ask your parents to forgive you when you hurt their feelings or when you disregard their wishes?

3. Read Luke 15:11–31 (The Prodigal Son)
   - Like the Prodigal Son, are you overly focused on your parents' financial status? Does this concern affect the way you interact with them?

- Have you begun to play financial games with your parents' estate in order to improve your inheritance? (Think of reverse mortgages, hiding assets prior to the Medicaid "look-back period," or getting overly involved in your parents' will and estate planning.)
- If you serve as your parents' power of attorney, are you acting prudently in their best interests, or are you tempted to find how you might personally benefit from future decisions?
- Are other siblings involved in your parents' financial management? If so, what is their role? What do you do if you disagree with your siblings?

4. Read Proverbs 20:20–21 (Do Not Curse Your Parents)
   - Are you able to hold your tongue from overtly criticizing your parents' decisions or their mannerisms when you are in public?
   - When you speak to your parents, are you verbally insensitive or condescending at times?
   - Do you think your parents feel respect from you, or might they feel that you are always looking down upon them with disrespect?
   - Do you constantly correct your parents when they are factually wrong, or can you let things go?
   - Do you grow impatient when your parents forget things or when they share the same stories repeatedly time and time again?
   - Are you sincere with your parents, or just play-acting to keep the peace?
   - Do you share your uncomfortable feelings with your parents, or do you stuff those uncomfortable emotions deep down inside?

5. Read Proverbs 23:22–25 (The Parent/Child Relationship)
    - Do you believe your parents are proud of you? Why? Why Not?
    - What have you done in your life that would lead your parents to be proud of you and joyful that they brought you into the world?
    - Are your parents disappointed in you? Why? Think of reasons for why they may find displeasure in your company.
    - Do your parents sometimes expect too much from you?
    - If you've had a rocky relationship with your parents in the past, how can you "start new" in their twilight years?
    - Are you proud of your parents? Why? Why not?
    - Do your parents embarrass you? Why? Why Not?
    - How can you cope with the occasional negative associations you make cognitively when thinking of your parents?

6. Read Proverbs 30:17 (Consequences for Disrespecting Your Parents)
    - Do you criticize your parents' mannerisms behind their backs?
    - Are you finding it difficult to value your parents and the relationship you have with them?
    - What can you do to create a healthier relationship with your parents?
    - What qualities of your parents do you greatly dislike? What qualities do you enjoy about them?
    - Have you asked for the Lord's Spirit to make you more accepting of your parents' faults and shortcomings?

2. Control

1. Read Job 23:1–17 (When Disaster Strikes)
   - Are you feeling as if you have lost control over your parents' end-of-life care?
   - Have you prayed for wisdom and guidance, or are you telling God how to run the show?
   - Do you feel your parents are getting a raw deal in life? Are they victims of bad circumstances? Are they suffering and deserve better?
   - Does it feel as if God is too passive and too quiet as you struggle to find order and meaning in your parents' final, hectic days?
   - Can you sense the presence of God during rough times, or do you feel all alone and detached from God?
   - Who is really in charge here?

2. Read Proverbs 3:5–8 (A Call to Trust in God)
   - What does it mean for you to trust in God with all your heart?
   - Can you live with uncertainty and ambiguity in your daily existence, or do you demand immediate answers and structure?
   - When was the last time you surrendered completely to God's will? What does surrendering mean to you? How can you accomplish that?
   - Do you believe that God will care for you, even if you let go of all control in your life?
   - Have you truly yielded to the will of God? Why? Why Not?

3. Read Isaiah 55:8–11 (The Omnipotent God)
   - Have there been times when you cannot make logical sense of events or circumstances? Are all events random, or are they predestined? Either way, is God in control?

- Do you believe that things happen for a divine purpose? Does God have a plan for your life? For your parents' lives? Or are you all on your own?
- Have you prayed to discern God's plan for you at this time in your life? How might that prayer sound to you?
- Do you pray for wisdom before making critical decisions, or do you rely on your own instincts or your own gut feelings?
- Are your parents' nestled safely in God's arms? Or is it all up to you to provide comfort for your parents?

4. Read Isaiah 43:1–3(a) (God Will Lead You through Your Troubles)
   - Are you able to find bright spots even in desperate times?
   - Whenever you are afraid, do you ask God to take you by the hand and lead you?
   - Do you believe that things usually work out in the end, or are you afraid of tragic endings?
   - How has God lifted you in the past? Will God protect you in the future?
   - When setbacks occur in your life, do you believe that God will pick you up again? Why? Why not?
   - Is there a limit to how many times the Lord can rescue you from danger?

5. Read Matthew 14:22–33 (Jesus and Peter Walk on Water)
   - When you step out of your comfort zone to help your parents, do you focus on the problems (scary waves?), or can you look to the Lord?
   - Do you have faith that the Lord will take your hand when you are afraid?
   - Do you worry incessantly, or can you push those worries aside and trust in God?

- Think of times when you metaphorically tried to walk on water by trying to accomplish too much? Were you successful on your own, or did God send help?
- Do you lose focus when your parents demand too much from you, or can you focus on God's providence?

6. Read Philippians 4:13 (You Can Do All Things in God's Grace)
   - When was the last time you felt overwhelmed by responsibilities and tasks? Did you ask God to help you?
   - Are there any problems that God can't handle?
   - Were there times in your life in which you rose to the occasion and performed even better than you initially expected? What happened?
   - Can you recall Bible stories in which weak men and women were strengthened by the power of God? Can God help you too?
   - Do you believe in miracles? Do they happen now, or were they limited to Bible times?
   - Is God capable of providing you with wisdom and understanding that you cannot obtain by your own efforts?

3. Guilt

1. Read Isaiah 55:6–8 (God Has Mercy on Those Who Repent)
   - Are you feeling guilty for ways in which you have mistreated or neglected your parents?
   - Do you believe that God can forgive you when you make mistakes?
   - How have you let down your parents over the years? Are they disappointed in you? Do you deserve their criticism?

- Do you believe you can make amends for transgressions of the past? How?
- Have you ever apologized directly to your parents when you've hurt them? Was it difficult? What happened? Did it improve your relationship?

2. Read Genesis 45 (The Joseph Story)
   - Think of times when your parents deliberately or inadvertently hurt you. Can you forgive them?
   - Is there unresolved anger in your family? Is anyone holding grudges? Why?
   - What would it take to resolve relationship hurts in your family? Have you prayed about this?
   - Have you considered making the first move to resolve any conflicts you currently have with your parents or with your siblings?
   - In your relationship with your parents, can you disagree with them and still express your love and affection?
   - If your parents have offended you, can you pray for the strength to let it go?

3. Read John 8 (Jesus Forgives the Adulterous Woman)
   - Whenever your parents offend you, can you offer forgiveness? Or do you want to retaliate?
   - Have you asked God to give you the strength to forgive others who mistreat you?
   - Have you been harshly critical of your parents' behavior? Do you fail to ask forgiveness for your own shortcomings? Is it possible to forgive and forget?
   - Do you ever keep score regarding your parents' faults? Do two wrongs ever make a right?
   - Can you take the high road and not repay evil for evil?
   - Can you pray, "Forgive us our trespasses *as we forgive* those who trespass against us"?

4. Read Matthew 5:11–12 (When Falsely Accused)
   - When your parents are nasty toward you, can you excuse them and walk away without holding any grudges? Or do you hold onto anger for a long time?
   - When your parents do not appreciate your kind gestures, how do you react? Do you decide to distance yourself from them in the future?
   - Do you believe this statement: "No good deed goes without punishment"? Why? Why not? Can you take "giving risks" even when your gifts may be rejected?
   - Do you tend to be too critical of yourself? Do you expect too much of yourself? Why? Why not?
   - When has God's grace comforted you during times when you were unfairly blamed or chastised? Can you think of specific times when you felt the unconditional love of God?

5. Read Luke 18:9–14 (Admitting Guilt)
   - In this story, with who do you most identify? The Pharisee or the tax collector? Can you swallow your pride and ask for forgiveness?
   - Can you humbly admit to your wrong doings, or do you make excuses by blaming others?
   - When your parents criticize you unfairly, do you speak up for yourself in defense, or do you take it on the chin? When would it be advantageous to self-defend? When would it be appropriate to just let it go? What words could you use to be tactful and diplomatic? Can you pray that God will give you the words to say during difficult times?
   - Has God offered forgiveness to you? To your parents? Think of examples.
   - Is there ever a sin that is unforgiveable? Which one(s)? Why?

- How often have you apologized to anyone in the past month? Do you find yourself apologizing frequently to others, or do you feel it is usually somebody else's fault when things go wrong?

4. Loss

1. Read Psalm 42:1–5 (Unlimited Tears)
   - Recall a few significant losses in your life. How did you deal with them? Have you given yourself permission to grieve and to cry?
   - Do you feel you've had more losses in your life than the average person? Or fewer losses? How do losses affect your faith and prayer life?
   - How has God helped you previously during times of loss?
   - Do you seek support from others during times of loss? Why? Why not?
   - Do you ever feel stuck in your grief or despair? If so, what can you do about it?

2. Read Psalm 34:18–19 (The Lord Is Near to the Brokenhearted)
   - During times of sorrow, how has prayer helped? Were you ever too upset to pray?
   - Do you believe that God will lift you out of your depression and sorrow?
   - How do you find hope in times of despair?
   - Can you think of ways you can offer encouragement to your parents who have had successive losses in their lives?
   - Will you consider attending a support group or talking to a therapist if you can't shake those feelings of loss and despair?

3. Read Psalm 121 (The Lord Watches over You)
    *   When times are rough, can you look "up" to God, or do you insist on looking "down" at the problems?
    *   Are there ways God can protect you from all harm and keep you safe?
    *   Has God provided hope and support through other people's words and deeds? Have you provided hope to others in their times of sorrow?
    *   Do you believe that God can bring recovery to any disaster?
    *   Have you prayed recently for strength and grace?
    *   Are you patient enough to wait for God to deliver you, or must the deliverance happen right away?

4. Read John 11:1–44 (Jesus Raises Lazarus from the Dead)
    *   Do you believe in life after death? Do you believe your parents will experience spiritual life after they die? If so, how do you envision that existence?
    *   Are you personally comforted by the Lazarus story? Why? Do you personalize the story, or does it seem like an event in the far distant past?
    *   Do losses leave permanent scars, or can people rise above their losses and find new joy?
    *   Has God ever blessed you with "new life" after a tragic loss? What were the circumstances involved?
    *   Do you believe that God can provide new "beginnings," or are we stuck permanently with the consequences of previous hurts?

5. Read Revelation 21:3–5 (God Makes All Things New)
    *   Can you embrace your parents' impending death as a form of new life?
    *   Can you perceive death itself as a form of healing?
    *   Do you ever feel guilty when thoughts of your parents' death bring relief to your soul?

- Is it ever inappropriate to pray for your parents to die?
- Have you ever prayed for your parents to leave this world forgiven, saved, and renewed by the grace of God?
- Are you able to discuss the topic of death freely with your parents, or do you shy away from the subject?
- Have you ever discussed advanced funeral arrangements with your parents, or is that subject taboo?
- Do your parents ever welcome death as a relief from the struggles of this world? If so, do you try to convince them otherwise? Why? Why not?
- If your parents do not believe in the existence of God nor in the existence of eternal life, how can you cope with that? What can you say to them?

5. Isolation

1. Read Isaiah 49:13–16 (God Will Never Abandon You)
   - Were there times in your life when you felt abandoned by God? When? Why?
   - Does verse 15 of this passage bring you comfort?
   - With God in your life, are you ever truly alone? Do you still feel alone even with the promise of God's presence?
   - Can you identify signs of God's presence in your life, either currently or in the past?
   - Have you prayed for the Lord to guide you and accompany you in your journey through life?

2. Read Psalm 27 (The Lord Is the Stronghold of Your Life)
   - Have other people ever abandoned you? Have friends ever deserted you? What about God?
   - Have you asked God to dwell in your life?
   - Is God far off and distant or close to your heart and soul?

- Does God keep promises? Can you think of biblical promises God has made and kept?
- Have you prayed for your parents to walk with God?
- Are your parents nonbelievers? If so, how has that affected the way you interact with them?

3. Read John 14:1–6 (Jesus Prepares a Place in Heaven for Us)
   - Do you believe that Jesus will keep the promise he made in John 14? Have you shared this promise with your parents? Do they know about Jesus' plans for them in the afterlife?
   - What if your parents reject the promise of everlasting life? Can you pray for them? With them?
   - What do you think heaven is like?
   - Can you envision a future reunion in heaven with those who have died before you? What does that look like to you?
   - Can you grasp the reality of heaven, or does it all seem too good to be true?
   - Have you ever worried about whether your parents will be in heaven some day? How have you addressed that concern with God and with them?

4. Read 2 Corinthians 1:3–7 (God Comforts All in Their Sorrows)
   - Do you believe that God feels your pain when you are alone or upset? Why? Why not?
   - Does it bring you comfort to know that you are not alone in your pain?
   - Can you identify friends, acquaintances, or professionals who can offer you comfort when you are feeling down? Have you opened up and shared your pain with them?
   - Have you considered attending a support group to gain insight, strength, and support from others who are struggling as you are?

- Have you thought about support persons who could help your parents deal with their painful issues and their challenging transitions?

5. Read Romans 8:28–35; 37–39 (Nothing Can Separate Us from God's Love)
   - Have there been times when friends are "not there" for you? How do you cope with their absence?
   - Do you believe the words of verse 38? If so, how do those words provide comfort for you?
   - Have you ever had a falling out with God? Have you ever felt as if you are losing your faith?
   - Are you willing to pray more often? How about praying when you feel alone and abandoned?
   - Do you think your parents feel isolated and alone? If so, how can you help to remedy the situation?
   - Are you able to pick up the phone and contact someone else for emotional support, or do you usually wait for others to make the first move?
   - Do friends constantly disappoint you when they are not loyal or not caring? Are you able to look past their shortcomings?
   - Have you asked for the Lord to help you seek out supportive people in your life?
   - Are you the primary or exclusive support person for your parents, or are there others who can provide nourishment too?

6. Anger

1. Read Matthew 21:12–13 (Jesus Expresses His Anger)
   - Are you able to express your anger, or do you keep it bottled up?

- Is anger a bad emotion or a healthy sign that something is wrong?
- Are you ever afraid of your anger as if it might get out of control? If so, what can you do to contain that rage?
- Do you ever explode in anger and then feel guilty later that you expressed yourself that way?
- What are some healthy ways to release anger?
- Have you ever walked away from an anger-producing environment and waited to calm down before reentering? How did that go?
- Do you ever pray for God to replace your anger with patience and understanding?

2. Read Ephesians 4:22–26 (Do Not Dwell in Anger)
   - When you get angry with your parents, do you dwell on the anger? Hold grudges?
   - Do you get angry often? How do you cope with your anger? In what ways have you learned to compartmentalize the anger so it doesn't spill over into other relationships?
   - How do you vent your anger? Do you yell? Pray? Talk yourself down?
   - Would you describe yourself as being angry most of the time? What changes can you make in your thinking to alleviate this problem?
   - When your anger goes away, does it stay away or return in waves? (Think of some examples from your experiences.)
   - How can God help you resolve your anger and find peace?

3. Read Exodus 32:19–26 (Moses Gets Angry at the Rebellious People)
   - Moses vented in a destructive way. Have you ever expressed anger in a destructive way? What happened? Did anyone get hurt?

- Aaron tried to talk Moses down from his anger. Are there people in your life who can calm you whenever you get enraged?
- When your parents provoke you to anger, are you able to pause and collect your thoughts before responding? Were there times when you were not self-controlled in dealing with your parents? Think of examples. Did you eventually find peace, forgiveness, and restoration? Why? Why not?
- Can you think of some nondestructive ways to burn off anger, such as exercise and prayer?
- Can your expressions of anger create positive outcomes? Why? Why not? Think of a few examples from your experiences.
- Have you ever alienated others by your angry outbursts?

4. Read Romans 12:17–21 (Do Not Seek Revenge When Angry)
   - Are you tempted to retaliate when someone unjustly hurts you? Can you let go of the pain?
   - Do you ever fantasize that bad things will come upon those who mistreat you?
   - Do your parents deliberately hurt your feelings with their words or rude behaviors? If they are inconsiderate of your feelings, is it intentional, or is it a sign of their own ignorance?
   - Have you ever tried to pray for your enemies as the Bible encourages?
   - When confronting your parents about an issue, can you speak the truth in love (Ephesians 4:15), or do you tiptoe around the issues so as to not incite their anger?
   - Have you ever sought an impartial mediator when in conflict with your parents over end-of-life care decisions?

5. Read Matthew 18:21–35 (Practice Unlimited Forgiveness)
   - Do you believe that a common antidote for anger is forgiveness?

- When your parents consistently fail to live up to your expectations, can you pray for the strength to forgive them?
- Do you pray for God to forgive you yet vehemently refuse to forgive those who hurt you?
- Can forgiveness be a gift you can give to yourself?
- How can you find peace in your heart when your expectations are not being met?
- Have you ever tried to lower your expectations for others when they constantly fall short of your demands?
- Is it easier to forgive others or to forgive yourself? Think of a few examples.
- Is forgiveness an option or a mandate from God?
- Have you ever asked your parents to forgive you for ways in which you might have hurt them?

7. Grace

1. Read John 14:27 (Jesus Promises Peace for Our Souls)
   - Do you believe that Jesus can bring you peace? If so, have you prayed for peace?
   - Can you designate certain times in your day for prayers that invoke divine peace?
   - It is possible to create space in your soul for peace? If so, what can you do to facilitate this?
   - How can you bring a peaceful demeanor and a peaceful environment to your aging parents?
   - How can you create a more peaceful environment at home? At work?

2. Read 1 Peter 5:6–7 (Cast Your Anxieties on God)
   - When you are anxious, can you pray for a calm soul?
   - Can you envision Jesus inviting you to share your burdens and troubles with him?

- Can you visualize the Lord holding you close in the way someone would comfort a child in distress?
- When anxious, can you refrain from excessive amounts of alcohol and/or medications?
- Do you believe that God listens to every prayer? If so, is it therapeutic to speak to God often?
- Can you still trust in God even when your prayers are not answered exactly according to *your* wishes?
- How can you help relieve the anxieties of your aging parents?

3. Read Psalm 91:1–4, 9–12 (God Will Lift You Up During Rough Times)
   - Can you trust in the providence of God according to verse 12?
   - Have you ever doubted God's ability to "carry" you? If so, how can you offset that doubt with faith?
   - Can you acknowledge the unlimited, saving grace of God in your life?
   - Are you willing to trust God completely with your future?
   - Have you opened yourself totally to the grace of God, or are you still clinging to your own ways of coping?

4. Read Ephesians 3:16–21 (Strengthened in the Assurance of God's Love)
   - Have you allowed Christ to dwell in your heart as stated in verse 17?
   - How can your life be different if you receive inner strength as mentioned in verse 16?
   - Can you appreciate the enormity of God's love for you in Christ Jesus?
   - Can you worship and adore the Lord even when you don't understand the Lord's essence or the Lord's ways?

- Can you believe that God will be faithful to you in your
  times of need?

5. Read Colossians 3:12–17 (Let the Peace of Christ Rule in
   Your Heart)
   - Can you find things to be thankful for, even when life
     is difficult?
   - When was the last time you truly counted your blessings?
   - Though life is stressful, can you see that blessings really
     do outweigh the problems?
   - Have you asked the Lord to "open the eyes of your
     heart" to perceive life through the paradigm of faith?
   - Are you able to identify the good qualities of your parents'
     lives and not dwell on the negative characteristics of
     their personalities?
   - When are you able to intentionally focus on the
     "positives" in life?
   - Are you able to believe in a brighter future, even if you
     can't see it yet?

Conclusion

In the Loving Arms of God

With a flair for symmetry, I conclude this book basically where it began: with my humble plea for you to let go and allow God to work out the fine details. Go ahead and experience the liberating joy of entrusting your future (as well as the future of your parents) to the ultimate, sovereign will of the Creator. In doing so, you will never be disappointed. God's wisdom far exceeds that of your own, so why not yield to the Almighty's "grace-filled" plan?

It Has Always Been about Control, Hasn't It?

Perhaps you are turning into somewhat of a control freak regarding your parents' end-of-life-care. If so, you are not alone. I am convinced that humanity has been created with a built-in need for control dating as far back as Adam and Eve. Just read the biblical narratives and you will encounter stories about several of God's children who desired ultimate control over their circumstances, over the environment, over other living creatures, over relationships, destiny, etc.

The etiologic narrative of Eden highlights humanity's desire to have complete power (i.e., to be "like God") and therefore to possess omnipotent control. In the Genesis narrative, Eve was tempted with words from the crafty Serpent. "For God knows that when you eat of it [the forbidden fruit] your eyes will be opened, and you will be like

God" (Genesis 3:4). Now follow the progression. In response to the Serpent's persuasive argument, Eve equated the consumption of the fruit with the acquisition of complete wisdom. For Eve, possession of this otherworldly wisdom was tantamount to having the very essence of the supreme Godhead.

The Serpent offered a lucrative proposal, and the fruit was there for the taking! Can you just imagine what Eve might have been thinking? *If I eat this fruit, I will have ultimate knowledge and control!*

Ironically, the first couple already enjoyed dominion over the earth, even prior to their consumption of the forbidden fruit. According to the narrative, the prefallen Adam was awarded custody of all creation by his benevolent God. He enjoyed absolute domain (control) over all living creatures, most notably his superiority over "the livestock, the birds of the air, and all the beasts of the field" (Genesis 2:20). Adam was given the authority to name the beasts and all living creatures—the very "naming" of the wildlife indicated his superiority, dominion, and control. But this earthly lordship did not quench Adam's thirst for *unlimited* control. There was a deeply ingrained quest for absolute power, and consumption of the forbidden fruit was perceived as the conduit through which such omnipotence could be transferred from the divine to the human realm.

It was also a desire for control that led Cain to murder his brother Abel (Genesis 4:9). Cain, motivated by an intense jealousy stemming from God's partiality to Abel's offering, reasoned that he could obtain absolute control of God's future blessings if only he could eliminate the one person who stood in his way: his brother. The murder was Cain's feeble attempt to gain control over the perceived powerlessness of the moment.

Countless other biblical narratives illustrate humanity's deeply ingrained desire for control, including these:

- the Tower of Babel event (Genesis 10–11)
- Abraham's desperate act to control his destiny by having relations with his Egyptian servant rather than trusting

that God would eventually provide an heir for him through Sarah (Genesis 16:4)

- Saul's consultation with a necromancer before battle in an effort to gain the upper hand when strategizing (2 Samuel 11)
- Delilah's craving for power over Samson (Judges 16)

There are many, many more examples—too many to illustrate within the scope of this book. As per the biblical testimony, *control* has always been, and will remain, a critical issue for humanity. The biblical witness verifies the undeniable reality of humanity's thirst for control and power. (After all, who really wants to be out of control?)

Therefore, consider this: any of your efforts to control your parents' future, (e.g., attempting to add more days or years to your parents' lifespan) may lead you to a crisis of enormous proportions when you realize that, for the most part, you only have limited control! Your parents are inevitably inching closer to their earthly finish line, and the clock keeps ticking as well. How can you prevent that natural progression? Obviously, you and the other members of the family system need to come to terms with the undeniable reality that death will come to your parents as it has come to all human beings since Adam and Eve.

No individual has discovered a way to thrive on earth in perpetuity. This means that no human individual possesses absolute, limitless power to prevent death, despite seemingly heroic efforts among some to achieve that goal. Mortal power becomes power*less* over the force of the Almighty, which, at the appointed time, beckons all flesh to its natural earthly end point. And so it bears repeating that *only God Almighty has absolute control over the living-dying interval.* The sooner we acknowledge this reality, the healthier we will be from a spiritual perspective.

The Bottom Line: Acknowledge the Omnipotence of God

To engage in anticipatory grief from a faith-perspective, one must continually affirm that God Almighty is in control. This theological perspective needs to be raised to the forefront or anxiety and frustration, very much an integral piece of the anticipatory grief experience, will escalate to crisis proportions for the dying parent and for those in relationship with the dying.

The theological reality of the omnipotence of God is played out in the Old Testament narrative of Job. In the Jobian narrative, the "victim" Job encounters all kinds of tragedies. His losses begin to multiply in geometric proportions. He loses his children, cattle, sheep, camels, dwellings, and ultimately his health and physical welfare. Is he dying? Perhaps.

At the onset of death and destruction, Job, in utter despair, is tempted to curse his God, to try to wrest control from this God of apparent injustice and tragedy, and to demand a logical explanation for the apparent injustices that have befallen him and his family. However, Job's *initial* response is an affirmation of the omnipotence of God! He acknowledges the sovereign authority of his Creator in stating, "The Lord gave and the Lord has taken away" (Job 1:20). Job realizes that circumstances are out of his direct control. He is simply powerless in the face of current disasters. In this ultimate statement of faith, Job declares that God is still in charge, even if circumstances and events do not reconcile with Job's perception of God as "just" and merciful. Job declares that God is in control, even though Job feels completely powerless in any effort to redirect the downward spiraling of his earthly demise.

Eventually, God Almighty answers the cries and troubling questions of the victim. The Almighty reminds Job that by divine rule and authority, the earth's foundation was laid (Job 38:4). The sea, sky, and land were formed by divine power (verses 5–11). Only God has seen the gates of death (verse 17). God Almighty controls the forces of nature and all living things (verses 22–41). And God has unlimited power and authority over the entire created universe (Job 40 and 41).

After God's lengthy monologue, Job acknowledges his powerlessness in the face of the Almighty. Job affirms the absolute authority of God while confessing his own mortal frailties. He states, "I know that you [God] can do all things; no plan of yours can be thwarted ... surely I spoke of things I did not understand, things too wonderful for me to know" (Job 42:2–3). How appropriate for Job to acknowledge that his God was, and is, still on the throne of divine omnipotence.

The biblical voice affirms repeatedly the absolute sovereignty of God. Proverbs 16:9 declares, "A man's mind plans his way, but the Lord directs his steps"; Isaiah 45:7 states, "I [God] form light and create darkness, I make weal and create woe, I am the Lord who does all these things." Elsewhere, it is written, "Thine, O Lord, is the greatness, and the power, and the glory, and the victory, and the majesty; for all that is in the heavens and in the earth is thine; thine is the kingdom, O Lord, and thou art exalted as head above all. In thy hand are power and might" (1 Chronicles 29:11–13). Psalm 147:5 states, "Great is our Lord, and abundant in power." Clearly, these verses and countless others affirm that God alone is the omnipotent ruler of all creation.

With all that in mind, you can choose between two options as you peer into the future. Either acknowledge and respect the sovereign will of God or attempt to take all matters into your own hands in a never-ending process of swimming against the current of destiny. Which of these options is better for you?

Who Is in Charge?

Anticipatory grief, if it is to be experienced from a faith perspective, must first and foremost acknowledge that there is no earthly ruler, no medical doctor, no oncology specialist, and no earthly guru who can compare with God. No mortal can stand up to God; no mortal can change the purposes and plans of the Almighty. This is most certainly true in the dying process.

The biblical witness reminds us that death itself is entirely in the realm of God's control. Psalm 104:29 states that it is God alone who "takes breath away" (ancient Hebrew descriptive metaphor for death). Psalm 146 clearly defines death as that time when humanity's plans must yield to God's ultimate purposes, and Ecclesiastes 12:7 indicates that, in death, the "spirit" (Hebrew *ruach*) returns to God *at God's appointed time* and in God's appointed manner.

The faith community has long understood the timing of death, aside from suicidal death, murder, or other killing brought about through the acts of human will, to be completely in the determining hands of God. This is a realization that all of us must acknowledge if we are to experience spiritual peace (in Jobian fashion). When your parents approach the time of their death, there is only one perfect prayer to utter: "thy will be done." This is a statement of faith that encapsulates an entire surrendering of the human will to that of the Designer of life and death itself!

What Are You *Really* Afraid Of?

I recently read a fascinating book authored by an Episcopal priest named Barbara Brown Taylor. The book's title speaks volumes: *Learning to Walk in the Dark.* Taylor indicates that most of us, since early childhood, were taught to fear the dark (literally). As we got older, we discovered other "dark" places that were spiritual or metaphorical in nature. True to form, we ran from those dark places just as quickly as we fled from the physical darkness when we were small children. However, as Taylor encourages, it is not a bad thing to journey into darkness, to lean into the abyss, and to learn more about God's saving grace, which is the same whether the environment is darkened or illuminated.[19]

Witnessing your parents' decline may be like journeying toward darkness. It is scary; it is unknown; it is not clear-cut in any way. Yet as Taylor advises, "Step 1 of learning to walk in the dark is to give up running the show"[20] If this directive sounds familiar to you, it may be because that option is what I have been encouraging all throughout this book: let go, and let God lead you through the darkness. Do not be afraid, but embrace what the darkness is trying to teach you about faith, trust, and the assurance of God's loving presence, even in those dark places of life and death, where you are feeling extremely powerless and vulnerable.

A Joyful Conclusion Awaits the Faithful

Death is not to be feared! In fact, Christians sing for joy in anticipation of a future heavenly reunion with the saints who have gone before them. There is no dreading the final chapter of life. In fact, there is an eager longing and expectation for what lies ahead. You may recall some of the traditional hymns whose lyrics remind us of the eternal bliss associated with those entering the heavenly realm.

> Rock of Ages, cleft for me,
> Let me hide myself in thee;
> ... While I draw this fleeting breath,
> When my eyelids close in death,
> When I soar to worlds unknown,
> See thee on thy judgment throne,
> Rock of Ages, Cleft for me,
> Let me hide myself in thee.
>
> —Augustus M. Toplady[21]

And recall the comforting words of lyricist Michael Joncas, as he reflects on Psalm 91.

> You who dwell in the shelter of the Lord,
> who abide in this shadow for life,
> Say to the Lord, "My refuge, my rock in whom I trust!"
> "And I will raise you up on eagle's wings,
> bear you on the breath of dawn, make you to shine like
> the sun,
> and hold you in the palm of my hand."
>
> —Michael Joncas[22]

The Christian community welcomes the day of victory when the souls of the departed are joined in heavenly celebration. In fact, for many, there is a feeling of excitement and sheer joy at the thought of arriving at the heavenly home sooner, rather than later, as expressed in these lyrics:

> Soon and very soon we are goin' to see the King,
> Soon and very soon we are goin' to see the King,
> Soon and very soon we are goin' to see the King,
> Hallelujah, hallelujah, we're goin' to see the King!
>
> —Andrae Crouch[23]

The anticipation resembles that of a young child eager for the arrival of Christmas morning. There is no fear, no anxiety, and no existential dread when contemplating the final breath of earthly existence. A similar feeling can be yours whenever you visualize your own parents crossing over from their earthly existence to the heavenly paradise! (Please note my description in chapter 4 when my mother was hours away from death. I reminded her that she would soon fall asleep but wake in the kingdom!). That thought sustained me through the difficult process of letting go and entrusting my mother to the eternal care of her Creator.

One of my favorite hymn lyrics (though seemingly not as popular as the lyrics just mentioned) tells of the joys ultimately experienced by those who have been "called home" to their eternal rest. In the twelfth century, Peter Abelard penned these words:

> Oh, what their joy and their glory must be,
> Those endless Sabbaths the blessed ones see!
> Crowns for the valiant, to weary ones rest;
> God shall be all, and in all ever blest.[24]

Christians believe that there is no human pain and suffering after death! What joy awaits those who will dwell in the heavenly kingdom.

In the Loving Arms of God

Take heart that heavenly paradise awaits those who take their final earthly breaths. God, in divinely gracious fashion, saves the greatest blessings for the final moments. Just think: someday your parents will enter their heavenly paradise, and you need not worry ever again for their safety or well-being.

I remind myself daily that, by the grace of God, my parents found their heavenly paradise. They may have occasionally kicked and screamed in protest during those days prior to God calling them home, but thanks be to God, they made it home—safely—into the loving arms of their Creator.

Someday, your parents will arrive at their eternal destination too. It may happen sooner than you expect, so why not choose *now* to make these final days rewarding and faith-filled for them— and for you? Do the very best you can as you gently usher your parents toward the sunset of their existence. Resolve to have a clear conscience and a grateful heart right to the end. Promise yourself that you will do everything in your power to nurture your parents today so that, when all is said and done, there will be no regrets lingering in your soul for years to come.

Go forward, by the grace of God, toward a truly faithful farewell. And may God grant you the peace and assurance of knowing that "God works for the good of those who love him ... if God is for us, who can be against us? (Romans 8:28, 31).

Amen!

Notes

Chapter 1

[1] "Thousands of Failures, but Thousands of Patents: Thomas Alva Edison," http://www.bukisa.com/articles/108679_thousands-of-failures-but-thousands-of-patents-thomas-alva-edison (June 13, 2009).

[2] Justin Zackham. *The Bucket List*, DVD. Directed by Rob Reiner (Warner Bros. Pictures, 2007).

[3] Elisabeth Kubler-Ross. *On Death and Dying* (New York: Macmillan Publishing Co., 1969).

[4] Ibid.

Chapter 3

[5] Henry Cloud and John Townsend. *Boundaries: When to Say Yes, How to Say No to Take Control of Your Life* (Grand Rapids: Zondervan, 1992).

[6] Robert Hemfelt and others. *Love Is a Choice: The Definitive Book on Letting Go of Unhealthy Relationships* (New York: Thomas Nelson, Inc., 2003).

[7] "You Can't Always Get What You Want." The Rolling Stones. Album: *Let It Bleed* (1969). Lyrics by Mick Jagger and Keith Richards.

[8] Lutheran Church in America, American Lutheran Church, Evangelical Lutheran Church of Canada, Lutheran Church: Missouri Synod. *Lutheran Book of Worship* (Philadelphia: Augsburg Press, 1978), 56.

[9] Rachel Snyder. "The Caregiver's Promise."

[10] *Father Knows Best*, television series (1954–1960). Created by Ed James. Starring Robert Young, Jane Wyatt, Billy Gray, Lauren Chapin, Elinor Donahue, et.al. 203 episodes, CBS.

[11] *Everybody Loves Raymond*, television sitcom (1996–2005). Created by Philip Rosenthal. Starring Ray Romano, Patricia Keaton, Brad Garrett, Doris Roberts, Peter Boyle, et al. 210 episodes, CBS.

[12] © Alzheimer's Association, 2011. Source unknown.

Chapter 5

13   Though the exact authorship of this prayer in unknown, its author is now generally identified as theologian Reinhold Niebuhr (1892–1971). The first verse of the prayer was publicly shared in 1937. Niebuhr is credited with adding the second verse as late as 1951. Text obtained from http://thevoiceforlove.com/serenity-prayer.html.

Chapter 6

14   Sammy Cahn. "Love and Marriage," music by Jimmy Van Heusen (Barton Music Corporation: ASCAP), recorded by Capitol Records, sung by Frank Sinatra, 1955.

15   Roman Krznaric. *How Should We Live?* (Katonah, New York: Blue Ridge, 2013), 265–266.

16   Ibid., 281–282.

17   Aging with Dignity, Inc. "Aging with Dignity," http://www.agingwithdignity.org.html.

18   Krznaric, 286.

Conclusion

19   Barbara Brown Taylor. *Learning to Walk in the Dark* (New York: HarperCollins Publishers, 2014).

20   Ibid., 15.

21   Augustus M. Toplady. "Rock of Ages, Cleft for Me," tune by Thomas Hastings in *Lutheran Book of Worship*, Lutheran Church in America and others (Minneapolis: Augsburg Publishing House, 1978). Hymn #327.

22   Michael Joncas. "You Who Dwell in the Shelter of the Lord." Lyrics and tune by Joncas in *With One Voice: A Lutheran Resource for Worship* (Minneapolis: Augsburg Fortress, 1995). Hymn #779.

23   Andrae Crouch. "Soon and Very Soon." Lyrics and tune by Crouch in *With One Voice*. Hymn #744.

24   Peter Abelard. "Oh, What Their Joy." Tune by Antiphoner in *Lutheran Book of Worship*. Hymn #337.

Bibliography/Suggested Readings

Theological Resources

Anderson, Ray. *Theology, Death, and Dying.* New York: Basil Blackwell Publishers, 1986.

Bailey, Lloyd R. *Biblical Perspectives on Death.* Philadelphia: Fortress Press, 1979.

Barth, Karl. *Church Dogmatics: Volume 3, Part 2.* Edinburgh: T & T Clark, 1960.

Becker, Ernest. *The Denial of Death.* New York: Simon & Schuster, 1973.

Cytron, Barry D. "To Honor the Dead and Comfort the Mourners: Traditions in Judaism" in *Ethnic Variations in Dying, Death, and Grief.* Washington, DC,: Taylor and Francis Publishers, 1993.

Dodd, CH. *The Background of the Fourth Gospel.* Manchester: Manchester University Press, 1935.

Doss, Richard W. *The Last Enemy: A Christian Understanding of Death.* New York: Harper and Row Publishers, 1974.

Gatch, Milton. *Meaning and Mortality in Christian Thought and Contemporary Culture.* New York: The Seabury Press, 1969.

Jungel, Ebergard. *Death: The Riddle and the Mystery.* Trans. by Iain and Ute Nicol. Philadelphia: Westminster Press, 1974.

Kierkegaard, Soren. *Fear and Trembling.* Ed. and trans. by Howard V. Hong and Edna H. Hong. Princeton, New Jersey: Princeton University Press, 1983.

_____. *The Concept of Anxiety.* Ed. and trans. by Reidar Thomte and Albert B. Anderson. Princeton, New Jersey: Princeton University Press, 1980.

Kubler-Ross, Elisabeth. *On Death and Dying.* New York: Macmillan Publishing Co., 1969.

Luther, Martin. *Luther's Works: Volume 51.* Philadelphia: Fortress Press, 1955.

Oden, Thomas. *Pastoral Theology: Essentials of Ministry.* San Francisco: Harper and Row Publishers, 1983.

Pattison, E. Mansell. *The Experience of Dying.* Engelwood Cliffs, New Jersey: Prentice Hall Inc., 1977.

Rahner, Karl. *On the Theology of Death.* New York: Herder and Herder, 1962.

Rupert, Hoover. *Where Is Thy Sting?: Death in Christian Perspective.* Nashville, Tennessee: Graded Press, 1969.

Taylor, Barbara Brown. *Learning to Walk in the Dark.* New York: HarperCollins Publishers, 2014.

Thielicke, Helmut. *Living with Death.* Grand Rapids: Eerdmans Publishers, 1983.

_____. *Being Human ... Becoming Human.* Garden City, New York: Doubleday Publishing Co., 1984.

_____. *Death and Life.* Trans. by Edward W. Schroeder. Philadelphia: Fortress Press, 1970.

Tillich, Paul. "Existential Philosophy" in *Journal of the History of Ideas: Vol. V.,* 1944.

_____. *Systematic Theology: Vols. 1,2, 3* in one collection. Chicago: University of Chicago Press, 1967.

Anticipatory Grief Resources

"A Comprehensive Analysis of Anticipatory Grief: Perspectives, Processes, Promises, and Problems" in Rando, Therese, ed. *Loss and Anticipatory Grief.* Lexington, Massachusetts: D.C. Heath and Co., 1986.

Krznaric, Roman. *How Should We Live?* Katonah, New York: Blue Ridge Press, 2013.

Kubler-Ross, Elisabeth. *On Death and Dying.* New York: Macmillan Publishing Co., 1969.

Medina, John J. *The Clock of Ages*. Cambridge: Cambridge University Press, 1996.

Mitchell, Kenneth and Herbert Anderson. *All Our Losses, All Our Griefs*. Philadelphia: Westminster Press, 1983.

Nathan, Laura. "Coping with Uncertainty: Family Members' Adaptations during Cancer Remission" in Clark, Elizabeth J. and others. *Clinical Sociological Perspectives on Illness and Loss*. Philadelphia: The Charles Press, 1990.

Nelson, Holly S. and Rodney J. Hunter, eds. "Dying Child and Family." *Dictionary of Pastoral Care and Counseling*. Nashville: Abington Press, 1990.

Nuland, Sherwin B. *How We Die: Reflections on Life's Final Chapter*. New York: Alfred A. Knopf Publishers, 1994.

Pattison, E. Mansell. *The Experience of Dying*. Englewood Cliffs, New Jersey: Prentice-Hall, Inc., 1977.

Rando, Therese A. *Grief, Dying, and Death: Clinical Interventions for Caregivers*. Champagne, Illinois: Research Press Co., 1984.

_____. *Loss and Anticipatory Grief*. Lexington, Massachusetts: D.C. Heath and Co., 1986.

Rosenberg, Morris. *Society and the Adolescent Self-Image*. Princeton, New Jersey: Princeton University Press, 1965.

Schoenberg, Bernard and others. *Anticipatory Grief*. New York: Columbia University Press, 1974.

Spiegel, David. *Living beyond Limits: New Hope and Help for Facing Life Threatening Illness*. New York: Times Books, Random House, Inc., 1993.

Liturgical Resources

Augsburg Fortress Publishers. *With One Voice*. Minneapolis: Augsburg Fortress, 1995.

Lutheran Church in America and others. *Lutheran Book of Worship*. Minneapolis: Augsburg Publishing House, 1978.

Helpful Websites

The Serenity Prayer: http://thevoiceforlove.com/serenity-prayer. html.

The Five Wishes Document: http://www.agingwithdignity.org. html.

Contact Jack

For more information about Pastor Jack, booking, and speaking engagements, go to

www.faithandfarewell.com

About the Author

Rev. Dr. Jack DiMatteo grew up in Phillipsburg, New Jersey and attended Rider University where he earned a BS in Accounting. After beginning a career at Coopers and Lybrand, Certified Public Accountants (then nationally ranked among the "Big Eight" firms in the field), he answered the call to ordained ministry and received his M.Div. degree from the Lutheran Theological Seminary at Gettysburg, Pennsylvania. Years later, Rev. DiMatteo engaged in further studies and was awarded a doctorate in pastoral theology from the Lutheran Theological Seminary in Philadelphia.

"Pastor Jack" has served as an ELCA Lutheran pastor in three New Jersey parishes: Dunellen, Keyport, and Budd Lake. For almost two decades he has been a hospice chaplain and spiritual counselor. After the September 11 national disaster, he was appointed by the Lutheran church to be the Director of Lutheran Disaster Response of New Jersey where he established support groups and financial grant assistance to those affected spiritually and financially.

Pastor Jack has also served as a college adjunct instructor in the areas of public speaking and philosophy. For a time he was a radio host of the show *Symphony of Praise* aired on WAWZ-FM, now known as "Star-99 FM", in Zarephath, New Jersey.

Pastor Jack currently resides in northern New Jersey with his wife Kathy. He has four children: Luke, Leah, Mark, and Michael.